WHY PEOPLE FAIL

WHY PEOPLE FAIL

The 16 Obstacles to Success and How You Can Overcome Them

SIIMON REYNOLDS

JOSSEY-BASS
A Wiley Imprint
www.josseybass.com

Published by Jossey-Bass
A Wiley Imprint
One Montgomery Street, Suite 1200, San Francisco, CA 94104-4594—www.josseybass.com

Jossey-Bass books and products are available through most bookstores. To contact Jossey-Bass directly call our Customer Care Department within the U.S. at 800-956-7739, outside the U.S. at 317-572-3986, or fax 317-572-4002.

Wiley also publishes its books in a variety of electronic formats and by print-on-demand. Some material included with standard print versions of this book may not be included in e-books or in print-on-demand. If the version of this book that you purchased references media such as CD or DVD that was not included in your purchase, you may download this material at http:// booksupport.wiley.com. For more information about Wiley products, visit www.wiley.com.

Library of Congress Cataloging-in-Publication Data
Reynolds, Siimon.
   Why people fail : the 16 obstacles to success and how you can overcome them / Siimon Reynolds.
       p. cm.
   Includes bibliographical references.
   ISBN 978-1-118-10617-4 (hardback); ISBN 978-1-118-16374-0 (paperback);
ISBN 978-1-118-12903-6 (ebk); ISBN 978-1-118-12904-3 (ebk); ISBN 978-1-118-12905-0 (ebk)
   1. Failure (Psychology)   2. Success–Psychological aspects.   I. Title.
   BF575.F14R49 2012
   158–dc23
                                          2011029151

Printed in the United States of America
FIRST EDITION

HB Printing   10 9 8 7 6 5 4 3 2 1
PB Printing   10 9 8 7 6 5 4 3 2 1

To my family: Tom, Jennifer, Guy, Hat, and Sam.
Thank you for a lifetime of love and support.

contents

introduction

There are thousands of books on success. But very few on failure.

Yet mastering failure is surely a vital step in achieving your aims, hopes, and dreams.

After all, success is often just a moment—a goal fulfilled, soon to be replaced with new goals. But failure is the ambitious person's constant companion, often dogging us for months, years, or even decades before we finally reach our aim.

We need to understand and conquer failure if we are ever to master success. You'd never know it from our education system. At school we're taught geography, history, mathematical formulas, and obscure scientific facts never to be used for the rest of our lives, yet how many of us, in all our years of formal learning, were ever taught how to overcome obstacles to any goal? Surely this is more important than all the other traditional school subjects put together.

Indeed, that is precisely what this book is about. In it I explore all the main causes of failure, in any field, and reveal solutions for overcoming them and creating a successful, happy life.

But who am I to be writing about this?

IF I CAN, YOU CAN

I wish I could say I was born a success, but the truth is vastly different. I performed very poorly at school. So poorly, in fact, that I remember several times my school principal hinted that I had little future there. I recall that at the bottom of one of my end-of-year report cards he even wrote, "If things do not improve, I think that Siimon had better leave the school." Ouch.

As you can imagine, those years weren't fun. But looking back on them now, I see that I could have excelled in class (and had a lot of fun at school) if I had only understood the principles of success and high achievement. It's those principles that I will reveal in this book.

The great turnaround in my life came when I made one momentous decision and stuck with it. That decision was simply that I would no longer put up with being mediocre, barely achieving anything noteworthy. I decided that I would become an expert at overcoming the kind of failure that had been shadowing me for most of my teenage years.

And so I began reading. One book, two books, 10 books, over time 100 books, then 1,000 books—on how to be a better, more successful person. I read biographies, motivational books, psychology manuals, science journals, anything and everything about how the human mind works and how I could make it work better.

Slowly I began to change. Old habits lost their controlling power; new habits gradually formed. I started getting better results at work and in my personal life. As you can imagine, as I began to see tangible changes in my circumstances I became even more encouraged and excited. Could it be that my future was actually in my own hands? Was it possible that I myself could create my life, rather than blaming my situation on other people and events or just plain old bad luck?

I became totally dedicated to studying the science of achievement and the art of personal fulfillment. I'm still studying success (and how to avoid failure) today, only now I have the good fortune to have made millions of dollars in my advertising career and have the freedom to do or be whatever I want.

So was I just lucky? I must say, although I have been lucky many times in my life, ultimately I think we make our own luck. At least in the long term. I believe I have arrived where I have in my career because I studied failure deeply and slowly worked out ways to get around it and clamber my way to success.

It wasn't easy. Lasting success never is. In fact, I reckon I have failed hundreds of times each year to achieve my aims. But by sticking to certain timeless strategies that I have learned from books, seminars, and bitter personal experience, eventually I have prevailed.

FAILURE LEADS TO SUCCESS

The most important message in the book is that failure leads to success. Even if you have experienced countless failures in your life, it doesn't mean you are destined to have success pass you by. If you learn the 16 principles in this book you'll be able to do more than turn your life around. You'll be able to uplift and transform it, taking it to levels that will amaze and delight you.

If I can, you can. I'm nobody special, but I've learned some special techniques and strategies that I'm incredibly excited about sharing with you in these pages.

Rest assured—success is a science. Long term it is highly predictable. No matter what field successful people excel in, no matter what time in history they ruled, ultra-achievers have performed a certain way and thought in a similar manner. In fact, the rules of success are so similar in every field of life that many people have excelled simply by copying the thoughts and methods of other high achievers in any field. As philosophers, spiritualists, and scientists have proclaimed for thousands of years, the earth is ruled by cause and effect. As one of the basic laws of physics states, "To every action there is an equal and opposite reaction." It is an ordered world in which we live, subject to ancient natural laws. Just as there are laws of gravity, motion, chemistry, and biology, so too are there laws of success and, inversely, definite paths to failure.

We need to learn the success laws. Study them. Master them. Then teach them to others. Because mastering these foundational life principles will bring us more wealth, achievement, and happiness than any university course or tertiary study.

STRATEGY IS IMPORTANT

Remember: if someone has achieved more than you, it's not usually because they are better than you or smarter than you. It's because they have discovered a better strategy for success. What they have learned, you can learn. What they have succeeded with, so too can you, if you learn the formulas of success. Some of these formulas are mental and others are practical and action oriented, but all of them can be mastered by those dedicated to the task.

Keep in mind that the human mind is an unfathomably awesome instrument. Almost everything we know about the brain has been discovered in just the last couple of decades. We have barely uncovered a fragment of the mind's potential, yet we already know that our brain is so powerful that it puts the world's largest mainframe computers to shame. We are super-beings, if only we knew it. But we need an instruction manual, a guide to how we can use our mind to create the most fulfilling life possible.

I'm certainly not suggesting that this book is a definitive summary of the human mind, but it is certainly a series of guideposts to show you how to experience vastly less failure and much more happiness in your life.

POWERFUL PRINCIPLES

The principles I share in the pages that follow have helped me enormously, and if you apply them diligently to your own life, they are sure to do the same for you.

Here's a brief review of some of the areas of failure I examine in this book.

In Chapter One, I look at the importance of developing a crystal-clear direction and purpose for your life. Most people simply do not have one. As motivational speaker Zig Ziglar famously remarked, "Most people are a wandering generality rather than a meaningful specific." This lack of clarity about our life purpose weakens our effectiveness to a massive degree. So, I look at some potent exercises to get you clear and motivated about what you most want out of your life.

In Chapter Two, I investigate the insidious damage that destructive thinking does to your psyche. I show you that such negative thinking is common in the mindset of a failure. Not only is destructive thinking disastrous for our chances of success, I provide evidence that it damages our health as well. I also reveal some simple ways to turn your thinking around and increase your sense of well-being and happiness markedly.

Next up, I look at productivity in Chapter Three. We all have the same 168 hours a week, but some people achieve enormous things in that time and others do little more than eat and sleep. Why? The answer, to a large degree, depends on how productive you are each hour of the day. You can be motivated, you can be intelligent, but if you are disorganized and ineffective in your actions then failure will be your close companion.

Actually, in my early to mid-twenties I was one of those people. Time and time again I let myself down with my lack of organizational skills and productivity systems. I have subsequently spent hundreds of hours studying the world's most respected time-management experts' works and integrated their best ideas into my life. It has made a crucial difference to both my success and my stress levels, that's for sure.

In Chapter Four, I reveal one of the biggest causes of failure in our society: fixed mindset. I show you research that proves that if you have this kind of mindset your chances of great success in life are small. But I also reveal an alternative mindset that will enable you to beat most of your competitors consistently. Apply this simple paradigm and your life will blossom in every area.

I delve into the importance of energy in Chapter Five. It's an often unappreciated aspect of success. But think about it: isn't it true that the person who has the energy to keep going is often the one who triumphs? Look at any high achiever and you'll see they have bountiful energy and verve. I share some really useful tips on how to boost yours.

In Chapter Six, I examine the dangers of not asking the right questions. The truth is, it's the quality of the questions you habitually ask yourself that determines the progress you make. Ask yourself shallow or negative questions and you'll get uninspiring answers. But train yourself to ask insightful questions and you can often turn around even major failures occurring in your life. I present you with a series of powerful questions I ask myself to overcome setbacks and problems that arise in my life. Make them a part of yours and you'll be amazed at how fast situations can improve.

Chapter Seven is all about poor presentation skills. They're a big reason people fail in their careers. You can have great content in your presentation, but if you don't present in a pleasing, confident, inspiring way many people will not treat you as a serious contender. Like it or not, people do judge by appearances. Are you sabotaging your success by presenting yourself physically, attitudinally, or verbally in a bad way? Don't worry if you are. I've got some easy ways to fix it and get you presenting superbly and making a major impression on the people around you.

What about your IQ? Do you think you score poorly in that area? Well, I show you important research that says that your IQ matters much less than most people think. What really counts is your EQ, otherwise known as emotional intelligence. Chapter Eight alone is enough to turn many lives around. Once you learn how to develop your EQ, your success level will leap dramatically.

Chapter Nine looks at self-image. It's very common for failures to have a poor self-image. When they look in the mirror they usually don't see someone highly competent and confident and an elite performer. No, they usually see themselves as a bit of a loser. Once anyone has a self-image that's not positive, it affects almost every area of their life. They try fewer things, take fewer risks. They don't take the inevitable rejections of life well and soon give up. They perform poorly socially. Alas, for people with a bad self-image, failure is just around the corner. But it doesn't have to be that way. Self-image can be changed, sometimes quite quickly. There have been mountains of research done in this area and in this chapter I give you some strikingly effective ways to boost your self-image.

Chapter Ten focuses on thinking. The fact is, life has become so busy that many of us spend all our time rushing around doing stuff, rather than balancing that action with constructive thinking. This is a terrible mistake. By simply learning to think more creatively more often, I believe you can transform the quality of your life. I have spent most of my career running the creative department of an advertising agency, so I've had to learn how to think up ideas fast. I show you some of my best thinking methods and give you tips on how you can use brain-storming to improve virtually any part of your life.

I focus on the amazing power of daily rituals in Chapter Eleven. Look at a failure in life and you'll always find that they do not follow consistent, life-enhancing rituals. They are unsystematic, up and down, and ever-changing in how they work and think. By establishing some basic supportive systems in your life, I'm certain I can increase your level of success, even if you're already a high achiever. After all, it's not what you do occasionally that builds your future—it's what you do regularly.

Chapter Twelve is all about the horrendous impact of stress on your life. It's a life crippler in so many ways. But if you're driven and ambitious, can you escape it? Not really. Some stress will be inevitable for anyone who's aiming for the stars. The trick is to manage that stress and even convert it into more motivation and achievement. You really can have success and peace of mind, and I'll show you how.

In Chapter Thirteen I examine how the quality of your interpersonal relationships affects your chances of failure. It's incredibly difficult to succeed at any endeavor on your own, and ultimately it's unfulfilling. Your network of business and personal relationships not only massively increases your chances of high achievement, it gives you an exceedingly valuable support system when the going gets tough—which at some stage it surely will. I've developed a simple yet highly effective system for enlarging and maintaining your set of relationships so that they support you in an optimum way.

In Chapter Fourteen I get into one of the biggest causes of failure in the world today: lack of persistence. It's a crying shame to see talented people so often fail for no other reason than that they gave up too early. The ability to continue toward a goal long after your enthusiasm for the journey has waned is at the very heart of a successful life. But society today promotes the quick fix, the shortcut, the easy money. Now more than ever in history, we are being tempted to move on to the next big idea rather than persist with our original aim. I know how tough it can be to keep persisting. I've struggled with it often in my life. In this section I give you the best methods I've developed to keep going when things are hard.

You may be surprised by the discussion on money obsession that follows in Chapter Fifteen. Am I really suggesting that being focused on money makes you less successful? You bet I am. Great achievements are rarely created by people just trying to get rich. Usually the titans of history were motivated by grander visions than just being able to buy a Ferrari. I discuss the limitations and dangers of money obsession and suggest some healthier alternatives.

Finally, in Chapter Sixteen I look at one of the primary causes of failure in life: not focusing on your strengths. It's an area too few people think about, but new research shows it's a crucial determinant of how far you go in life (and how much you enjoy the journey). Most people hardly spend any time each day doing what they are good at and love. As a result, their performance is often average and their motivation low. It's hardly a prescription for success. In this chapter I provide you with a questionnaire that can quickly help you get clear on what your primary strengths are (most people don't know) and give you some pointers on how to spend much more time each day doing stuff that you're excellent at and that delights you.

HOW TO READ THIS BOOK

The best way to digest this book is to first read it through, beginning to end. Then pick the three areas of failure that you feel most apply to you. Reread those chapters with a pen and paper handy and make notes and observations about your feelings and past experiences relating to those issues.

Finally, pick just one principle that you feel is most relevant to your life at the moment and make a commitment to conquer this aspect of failure. Write a list of ways you can overcome this obstacle and stick it up where you can see it each and every day, both at home and at work. Then do something, anything, every single day for a month to master it.

After you've conquered that area of failure, move on to the next of your top three failure challenges. This single-minded focus will ensure that meaningful improvements in your life will occur within weeks, even days. The mere fact that you are concentrating your focus on just one area at a time to improve will guarantee swift change. Concentrated effort works.

Finally, get excited. You're about to discover countless ways to avoid failure and maximize your success. Many people have entirely changed the course of their lives by mastering just one of the timeless principles in this book. Improve on five or ten of them and your life will rocket to a totally new level. You are soon to learn the master skills of ultra-achievement, skills you'll be able to use for the rest of your life to increase your wealth, success, contentment, and happiness.

I believe human beings are designed to grow, improve, and excel. Our possibilities are virtually endless. All we need are the instructions on how to unlock our mighty powers.

This is that instruction book.

WHY PEOPLE FAIL

unclear purpose

Here's the truth about success: You don't have to be smarter than everyone else, or better looking, or more connected, or luckier to make it big in life. You just have to focus—really focus—on what you want and how you can get it.

The reality is that most people are really quite unclear about their desires for life. Sure, they want to be successful, sometimes very much, but when you ask them the how, what, who, and why of their purpose they are usually foggy about the details.

The average person has no clear purpose, and that's why people end up average. But very occasionally you'll find individuals who are not necessarily brighter than their competition but much more clear about what they desire, who they want to be and where they want to go. And they are the ones who make it in the game of life.

I went to a very academically oriented school—in fact, some of the most intelligent teenagers in the state were students there. But curiously, many of the best and brightest minds didn't end up excelling in later life. They were overtaken by other people who may not have been as intellectually bright but who had a strong sense of where they were going, took daily small steps to get there, and ended up ahead.

It reminds me of that science experiment we used to do in school. Remember using a magnifying glass to burn paper? You could leave a piece of paper in the sun all day and it would be almost unaffected by the sun's rays. But concentrate the sun's rays with a magnifying glass and within a few seconds the paper would be on fire. That's the power of focus. People with a clear purpose are far more focused than the majority of the population, and the results show in every area of their lives.

There are three areas where you need to be absolutely clear about your purpose.

LIFE PURPOSE

If I asked you, "What is your life purpose?" what would you say?

Do you have an overall philosophy of life, a primary reason you get up every morning? Or are you just pulled along by current events, deadlines, and people asking you to do things?

Amazingly, most people can't articulate what their life purpose is. They literally have no reason that they are here on the planet. As a result there is little dynamism in how they live. They coast through life, looking for the next small pleasure and trying to avoid any possible pain. They are rudderless. Often not miserable, but not bursting with optimism either. If that describes you, let me give you a few ideas about what your purpose in life could be. Take a look at the following list and see if any of these possible life purposes strikes a chord with you.

Possible Life Purposes

To create a beautiful, happy family
To become an outstanding human
To be a master of my field
To have a series of enriching relationships
To make a major contribution to humankind

To change the world
To help as many people as possible
To be a great friend
To reach a high spiritual level
To have amazing adventures
To leave a legacy
To enjoy every day

If none of these fits your vision for your life, take a minute or two to write three possible life purposes that appeal to you.

It doesn't really matter what your life purpose is—it just matters that you have one. Why? Several reasons, actually.

A great life purpose inspires you. It gets you up in the morning. It excites you. It involves you in life. It enriches your existence and that of those around you. It makes life more interesting, more fun, more adventuresome. When times are tough, the inspiration you get from your life purpose pushes you to overcome any adversity in pursuit of your life goal.

A great life purpose makes you more effective. Instead of wandering around in a daze, having a strong life purpose clarifies your life, makes you focus on what you have to do and how to do it. It keeps you from being lazy and performing at a low level. It gets you up early in the morning, working on making the vision for your life a glorious and fulfilling reality.

A great life purpose makes you grow. Just attempting to fulfill your life mission unlocks many of your latent powers. It stretches you out of your comfort zone, encouraging you to go beyond what you may have thought you were capable of. It awakens you to your higher potential and makes you feel truly alive. A great life purpose can be the impetus for substantial self-improvement, even self-revolution.

With all these great things arising just from having a life purpose, isn't it absolutely extraordinary that so few people have one?

If you do only one thing suggested in this book, make it this. Decide what you want your life purpose to be, commit to it emotionally in your heart, then put up a reminder where you can see it every single day. As you begin focusing on your life purpose daily, you will see your life quickly transform and become simpler and more gratifying. You will have direction and unstoppable momentum. And believe me, the people around you will sense it.

After defining your life purpose, the second type of purpose you need to achieve clarity on is your job purpose.

JOB PURPOSE

Once again, it is astonishing how unclear most people are about exactly why they're employed.

In the next 30 seconds, please write below what your three most important tasks are at work. If you're a stay-at-home mom or dad, make it the top three at home.
Now number them in order of priority, 1, 2, and 3.

If you're typical of the majority of people I give this quiz to, the answer won't come immediately. You'll probably have to think for quite a while to work out what the correct order is, too.

However, if you immediately listed your most important job tasks, the ones you're really paid for, then congratulations—you've got a crystal-clear job purpose. If you couldn't do this, then it's definitely worth taking the time. Because once you're clear on your top job tasks, you'll immediately start doing your job better. You'll waste less time, finish tasks sooner, get better results more quickly. Such clarity creates extraordinary power and momentum and much greater vision. When you're absolutely clear about the three most important tasks in your work life, it shows. You won't accept time wasters, you'll work more effectively, you'll get things done with a minimum of fuss, and people will respect you for your inner centeredness.

Vagueness Leads to Failure

Compare staff members who have total clarity of purpose with those who have only a vague idea of what their job is. The latter will be less motivated, far easier to distract, less efficient, and less effective. They'll spend loads of time on unimportant tasks, as if they have nothing better to do. (In their view, they don't.) They'll be happy to attend trivial meetings and take long lunch breaks, because there's nothing in particular driving them to succeed.

Surely one of society's greatest diseases is the overwhelming number of tasks we must do every day. An avalanche of e-mails, a maelstrom of meetings, endless To Do lists—these days it never stops. Work life is more intense than ever. But because there is always so much that needs doing, the person who isn't clear on his or her top job priorities can easily get caught up doing the endless trivial tasks we are all bombarded with every day. That person majors in the minor things.

It's not unusual to see people working 12 hours a day and still not getting anything substantial done. Why? At the heart of it, their lack of clarity about the best use of their time leads them to work on what's urgent, not what's important. Time-management excellence (which we will cover at length in Chapter Three) begins with total clarity about your ideal outcomes. Foggy purpose always leads to mediocre results, no matter how intelligent you are. In fact, if I had to choose between a person of average intelligence who was working with a clear purpose and a brilliant one who had no clear purpose, I would bet on the average person to win every time.

Which brings us to the third level of purpose—being clear on what your weekly purpose is. This is such a simple idea, but it can revolutionize your level of achievement.

WEEKLY PURPOSE

All that your weekly purpose involves is being disciplined about sitting down once a week, often on a Sunday, and thinking about the one or two most important tasks for the following seven days. It's a terrifically powerful exercise that takes only a few minutes but can lead to a sizable improvement in personal effectiveness. Very often, once the week begins we get caught up in all the activities of life. Then Friday evening comes and we look back and realize we haven't achieved anything of note. We've just done lots of unimportant things—sometimes to a high standard, but as investment guru Warren Buffett likes to say, "What is not worth doing, is not worth doing well."

But make the weekly purpose a habit and you'll be much more likely to achieve at a high level. Once you're really clear about the week's über-important task, your mind tends to return to it again and again until it gets done. You'll focus on any task that's related to it, while avoiding irrelevant jobs and trivial to-dos.

The weekly purpose is also a great barometer of whether you've had an effective week. Each weekend, simply ask yourself whether you got those top two jobs done. If you didn't, then to be brutal, you failed your week's mission. If you did, well then, congratulations. You're a top performer.

In some respects, high achievement is very easy. If you did just *one* important task each week you could achieve 52 important tasks a year. And you can make a lot of progress taking 52 big steps toward any goal, that's for certain.

Try the weekly purpose process this weekend, and I think you'll experience a quantum leap in your efficiency. Do all three purpose exercises and your speedy progress will astound you.

(To watch a free video where I discuss the Power of Purpose, visit www.whypeoplefail.org.)

THE REMARKABLE RAS

These techniques work so well because they help your brain process information far better than it can when you are not clear about your key purposes in life. This is largely due to a part of your brain called the reticular activating system. To me the RAS, as scientists like to call it, is one of the most exciting parts of the brain. Let me explain why with this little three-step test.

Take 15 seconds and look around the room you're in at this moment.
Now memorize the location of anything that is black in color. Do that now before reading the next step.
Right, now without looking around the room again, see how many objects you can remember that are blue, white, or brown.

You'll find it very hard to name any at all, even though your eyes passed over them several times. The reason you can't is largely because of your brain's RAS.

The RAS works like this: because there are billions of pieces of information in the world, your brain has to choose which of them are useful and which aren't. For instance, if you're a keen tennis player your RAS will pick out articles in the newspaper about tennis, notice advertisements for tennis matches, or spot tennis shows on TV, even out of the corner of your eye. Because you've programmed your brain's RAS that tennis is important to you, it dutifully goes to work to bring you tennis-related data.

But imagine if you had no clear purpose for your life, your job, or your week. How could the RAS help you spot opportunities and see stuff of relevance for you? It couldn't. A wishy-washy purpose prevents the awesome power of your brain's RAS from assisting you to achieve what you desire. It dramatically reduces your ability to move toward your ideal life.

Most people don't know about the RAS, so they miss out on using its incredible computing power to help them get what they want. Now that you do know about it, be sure to take the time to tell your RAS what you want clearly, so it can help you find what you're looking for in your life, job, and week.

YOUR BRAIN IS YOUR ALLY

Your brain is designed to assist you in the most extraordinarily powerful ways. But if you never give it clear instructions about what you're seeking in life, it will struggle to help you make progress. As the saying goes, "If you don't know where you're going, any road will take you there."

Clarity leads to greatness. In fact, a clear purpose is an absolute prerequisite for excellence in any aspect of your life. I guarantee that if you are having long-term trouble in any area of your life, it is because of uncertainty about your real purpose in that area.

The power of clarity is absolutely stupendous. It really is one of the primary determinants of the level of success and happiness you'll reach in your life.

With that in mind, it pays to go even deeper with your life clarification. This won't be time-consuming, either. Just grab a clean sheet of paper and a pen and I'll show you how to get greater clarity on your life than you've probably ever had before, in just minutes.

I call these next exercises "The Three-Minute Masterplans," because in only three minutes you can take a good look at your life and get absolute clarity on what you want.

1. Ideal Person Clarity

Now, while you're on a roll, take three minutes to brainstorm your ideal person clarity. This one's all about you. What type of person would you really like to be? What's your ideal personality? Are you noble? Confident? Efficient? Relaxed? Spiritual? Joyful? Write down five character traits you wish you possessed. Remember: you don't have to think deeply about it, just jot some thoughts down. You can always change them later.

Now take a look at that list. You should find that ideal person inspiring. You should even feel a little excited at the possibility that you could become that type of human. Well, I can promise you this: if you read that list each morning and train yourself to think about those characteristics several times throughout the day, you will inevitably begin to become that person. It is one of the great truisms of life that we become what we consistently think about. But you must first be clear about the type of human you wish to become.

2. Life Partner Clarity

If you're single but don't want to be, take three minutes to write down all the character traits you'd like in your ideal partner. Don't think too much about the traits, just write them down fast. Aim to list at least five. In no time at all, I bet, you'll be much clearer on what your ideal partner is like—his or her appearance and behavior, and what he or she stands for in life. Having that clarity in your mind will give you a much better chance at recognizing such a person when you meet him or her. It will also make clear who is not right for you.

3. Friendship Clarity

Finally we come to the third three-minute exercise, focusing on friendship clarity.

It's a fact that we become like the people we hang out with. As the saying goes, "You lie down with dogs, you get up with fleas." The people around you affect you in more ways than you may think at first. Slowly, subtly, almost imperceptibly, your attitudes start to become like theirs, your actions begin to be in accordance with their way of thinking. Then before you know it, you've adopted many of your friends' beliefs and ways of behaving.

That's why it's so imperative that you choose your friends carefully. Each of them should display at least several character traits that you admire. But what exactly are the traits you most admire in a friend? The truth is, most people have never thought about it. Their group of friends just happened—they didn't consciously choose them. As a result, the quality of some of those friendships is poor. And poor-quality friendships usually lead to a low-quality life.

Take three minutes now to write a list of five character traits you'd like your friends to have.

Once you review the list, you'll probably realize that a few of your friends don't really make the grade. They are lacking almost all of the traits you'd like in a good friend. Possibly you became friends almost by accident, and remained friends largely because of habit. Well, maybe it's time to cease the friendship.

Now don't get me wrong—I'm not suggesting you terminate important friendships just because your pals aren't "ideal people." The truth is, you may get along fantastically with them and greatly value your time together. But I am asking you to take an honest, hard look at your friends and ask yourself this question: are these the type of people I really want to spend the rest of my life hanging out with?

If the answer is no, then you should consider seeing less of them and spending more time each month looking for the kind of friends you know (deep down) you deserve.

TOUGH DECISIONS

These exercises present challenging issues, I'm sure you'll agree. But isn't it interesting that it was only when you got some clarity about your friendships that you even questioned your friends' qualities? Without getting clear about what we deserve in every area of our lives, we all tend to just put up with mediocrity.

So with that in mind, I have another question for you: is there any other area of your life that you're a bit foggy about? Even if you take just three minutes, get clear on what you want in that area. That's often all it takes. You'll be amazed at how quickly you can clear up any greyness you have about an issue when you consciously focus on it. This technique is simple and effective.

Once you've created all these lists, you must stay reminded of them. Otherwise, you'll end up slipping back into your old habitual ways of operating. A good way to keep them in mind is to write each of your Clarity List answers in a journal and spend a minute or two each day reading through them and reflecting a little on whether what you're getting in these areas is what you're wanting.

The simple truth is this: the more clarity you have about what you want in every area of your life, the more likely you are to get what you want.

Clear?

destructive thinking

There's a killer in your home tonight.

Not a killer of people, but a killer of dreams, achievement, and all manner of success. This killer is invisible, yet its deadly work can be seen everywhere: in careers, in relationships, in people's health, and certainly in their minds.

That killer is destructive thinking.

Long term, I do not believe there is a single factor more detrimental to a successful life than the habit of thinking destructively. It has an incredibly adverse effect on virtually every aspect of your life. What makes it even more potent is that in our society today few people respect its monumental power. Most of us simply don't take seriously how we think.

Take, for instance, the common reaction to people who try to do the opposite of destructive thinking—positive thinking. Often people quietly ridicule positive thinkers as dreamers, naive optimists who are kidding themselves about the real state of the world. Many assume positive thinking is ineffective at best and harmful at worst. In this chapter I hope to show quite the opposite—that optimistic thinking is one of the most powerful techniques you can use to avoid failure in life, as long as you practice it consistently.

The truth is that the quality of your thinking has a gigantic impact on the quality of your life, and if you only realized this you would devote time every single day to strengthening your mental state.

That's right—I'm suggesting a mental fitness regime just like many of us have a physical fitness regime. A ritual that can be performed simply and easily every morning and evening that keeps your mind away from destructive thoughts, or at least stops your dwelling on them. Negative thinking is just too darn powerful not to be combated daily.

Let's take a look at some of the effects of destructive thinking.

DESTRUCTIVE THINKING AFFECTS YOUR HEALTH

Numerous studies have shown a correlation between negative thinking and illness. One that particularly struck me was an investigation into the mental state of breast cancer victims. Dr. O. Carl Simonton interviewed around 400 women with breast cancer and discovered that in over 80 percent of the cases, the women had suffered a devastating negative event around nine months prior to discovering the illness.

Now am I suggesting that all cancer is caused by sad or negative thinking? Absolutely not. Clearly, many types of cancer have a genetic component. But am I saying that I believe destructive thinking (in this case arising from a negative event) can weaken a human's immune system? You bet I am.

Respected positive psychology pioneer Dr. Martin Seligman talks of a fascinating research study on positive thinking and health involving the life expectancy of nuns. Believe it or not, nuns make excellent research subjects, because everyone in a convent eats mostly the same thing, does mostly the same activities and lives in the same protected environment. As such, they provide a very pure sample for research tests.

In his brilliant book *Learned Optimism*, Dr. Seligman reports a research study in which new nuns were asked to write a letter describing how they viewed their life in the convent. After 50 years the researchers reviewed the nuns' letters, comparing each letter with its author's life span. They found an astounding result. Almost every nun who had described her convent life negatively in her letter had had a shorter life span than the nuns who had written positively about their lifestyle. Seligman argues that the character trait of negativity in a nun's youth was likely to have continued throughout her life and was also likely to have shortened her life.

Both the Simonton and Seligman studies are remarkable, but they are just two of many conducted over the last twenty years that support the theory that negative, pessimistic, or destructive thinking has an extraordinary impact on our health.

There's plenty of evidence to show that happy thoughts make us healthier, too. Here's one of many stories that supports the notion.

In the now classic book *Anatomy of an Illness as Perceived by the Patient*, Dr. Norman Cousins wrote a detailed account of how he cured himself of a rare degenerative disease by making himself watch funny movies for hours on end. Cousins fervently believed that by staying upbeat and positive, he strengthened his body's ability to ward off the disease.

Twenty years after that book's publication, the field of psychoneuroimmunology (or how the mind affects the immune system of the body) has become a fast-growing school of medical research. Where once doctors scoffed at the thought that our thinking affects our body's cells, now tens of thousands of them accept that the two are intimately connected.

Let's now move on to another ugly result of thinking destructively.

DESTRUCTIVE THINKING MAKES YOU WANT TO GIVE IN

To me this is a self-evident fact. If I am trying to reach a major goal but deep down I don't really think I will achieve it, then I am much more likely to give up at the first sign of an obstacle or hardship. After all, why flog myself to reach a seemingly unreachable goal?

Compare this attitude with that of an optimist. Optimists believe passionately that they will achieve their goals, almost irrespective of how many bumps they encounter along the road. As a result they keep persisting and pushing until finally they achieve what they set out to do. It's entirely logical.

In my opinion people who don't believe in the power of positive thinking simply have not properly considered the connection between our thinking and our likelihood of persevering until we triumph. This relationship between thought and outcome is best summed up by the simple diagram here.

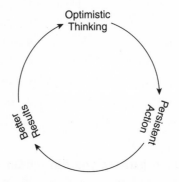

Expressed in words, the diagram says that your thinking affects what actions you take. Those actions then give you some kind of result, and then the result changes how you think. There is a direct connection between your thinking and your actions; therefore, the quality of your thinking is exceedingly important to reaching your final goal.

Top sports psychologist Gary Mack talked of an experiment on the power of the mind that he regularly carried out when he coached professional sports teams.

First he got all the athletes to stand up. Then he asked them a simple but important question: "Who believes that their performance on the sporting field is affected by how they think, by at least 50 percent?" He reported that at least half the room agreed.

Mack then asked a very powerful question: "If most of you believe that your state of mind changes your final performance so greatly, why aren't you spending 10, 20, 30 or even 50 percent of your training time on thinking in the right way?" The room was usually silent, because it had suddenly occurred to these professional sportspeople that they were not devoting nearly enough time to mind training for peak performance.

THINKING AFFECTS ACTIONS

Remember: your thoughts change your actions, then your new actions give you new results. Make the effort to think optimistically and you are far more likely to keep moving toward your goals, even when things get tough. Think destructively and you will be more inclined to give up when the inevitable obstacles arise. It's obvious, but we often forget it, don't we?

Many people believe that their thoughts are truth, but in reality they are just the mechanistic actions of the brain: an event happens, and you have a thought about it. It's not necessarily the truth, it's your perception of the truth, and it may or may not be accurate. If you habitually perceive events negatively, you can retrain your mind. You don't have to continue thinking a certain way—with commitment, you can change how you think. You can improve it, uplift it so that your thinking supports you, rather than pulls you down into mediocrity and sadness.

Look at depression patients. There are hundreds of millions of people suffering from depression, but typically their way of thinking has several commonalities. Numerous studies have shown that many depressed people have three defining characteristics of thought.

1. *They believe their problems are personal.* When a bad event happens to a depressed person, they often take it personally. They believe it's their fault, or that that they personally are responsible and even worthy of blame.

2. *They exaggerate the size of the problem.* Usually someone gets depressed when they make a "problem" seem huge and insurmountable. When they make the problem big in their minds they can barely muster the energy to even address it, let alone conquer it. Depressed people are usually overwhelmed by their situation and believe it's too big for them to address effectively.

3. *They believe the problem is permanent.* Time and time again, studies show that depression patients cannot see an end to their predicament. In their view the obstacles they face are likely to be with them for ages, or even forever. This gives them a terrible feeling of hopelessness.

So we can see that depressive thinking doesn't just happen: in many cases, there's usually a specific way of thinking that brings it on. And for a multitude of other moods we get it's a similar situation—specific thinking patterns create specific moods.

That's why it's so important to guard your thinking, to keep yourself from slipping into destructive thinking patterns. By taking charge of your mind you can direct it to perform in a more effective manner. You must remember that you rule your brain, not the other way around.

THE DAILY MIND RITUALS

With that in mind I'd like to now introduce you to the daily ritual I use to keep myself in good shape mentally.

The SCORE Technique

Throughout the day I use two main techniques: SCORE monitoring and the Breath Release. The SCORE technique was created by Jim Fannin, one of the world's finest high-performance coaches. He has been refining this technique for over twenty-five years and I can vouch for its effectiveness. In a nutshell, it works like this. Throughout the day, each time you are about to go into a meeting or perform a new task, take a few seconds to monitor yourself in the following areas.

Self-discipline. Ask yourself whether you're working toward your goals, doing what you know you should be doing in a disciplined manner.

Concentration. Check whether you are focused and concentrating on the task at hand.

Optimism. Are you enthusiastic, energetic, and positive? Are you expecting things to go well?

Relaxation. Check your tension: make sure you're not too uptight, that you're calm and relaxed but not lethargic.

Enjoyment. Monitor your enjoyment levels. Make sure you're feeling good and appreciating the moment. Ensure that you're choosing to have fun with whatever you're doing.

As you've probably worked out, the first letter of each of these words forms the word SCORE. It's Fannin's experience that when these five facets of your mind are in good shape, you are functioning mentally at a super level. You are in that special mental space that athletes call "the zone." It only takes a few moments to monitor yourself in these areas each time you move to a new task throughout the day, but in my experience it really works. Try the SCORE system for just one day and I'm sure you'll agree that it keeps you sharp and positive.

The Power of Breath

I call the second mind technique I use each day the Breath Release, and it's as effective as the SCORE technique.

It's based on the theory that throughout the day we encounter numerous little mental stresses that store themselves inside our body. These can be released with breathing exercises, just like physical tensions can be released through a massage.

The technique is really simple. Several times a day, when you have a spare moment or two, take a few moments to think about whatever has stressed you. Then take a deep breath and as you breathe out, imagine that the stress is leaving your body. Visualize the tension leaving you as you slowly exhale. Then on each new inhalation imagine you are being filled with calm and joy.

Try it once, right now. It's a remarkably effective technique. When you release your stress numerous times through the day, you'll usually find that by the end of the day you hardly feel stressed at all. But if you don't regularly release the tension of the day it will almost inevitably rise inside you, making you feel uptight and on edge by the time the sun goes down.

It's the belief of many stress experts that it's because we let tension (mental and physical) develop inside us over the years that our health begins to break down. Certainly anyone who has read the works of the famous heart doctor Dean Ornish will be acquainted with the medical research that links heart disease to ongoing stress. It's not a huge leap to assume that cancer is affected by unreleased stress as well.

That's why the Breath Release technique is so powerful. It stops development of major stresses by nipping them in the bud early when they're just beginning to arise.

Breathing deeply together with the SCORE technique are the two mental strategies I use all through the day. Typically I'll do each technique five to ten times a day, depending on how busy or how stressed I am. Believe me, they make a huge difference to my mood and performance.

Next we come to the mind exercises I do in the morning only: visualization and affirmations.

Visualizing

Visualization is simply seeing a picture in your mind. Visualizing yourself performing perfectly (mentally rehearsing in your mind's eye your life going smoothly) is an exercise you repeat 10–50 times, over a few minutes or so.

This is how I do it. In the morning before work I put on some inspiring music and settle into a comfy chair, close my eyes, and relax. I then spend 20 minutes listening to the music and imagining myself performing superbly at work, at the gym, socially—any area that I care about. I replay the scenes of my perfect performance in my mind again and again and again until I can easily see myself (and believe myself) performing at the level I've always dreamed of.

When I started doing this visualizing it felt a little strange, I must admit, but now I'm very comfortable doing it. In fact, it's one of the most enjoyable activities in my day.

Visualization has been used for thousands of years by Indian yogis to enhance their powers, but since the East German Olympic team pioneered its use in modern sport in the 1960s, it has become a vital part of many pro sports teams' training systems. And with good reason— countless research studies have shown that athletes who consistently visualize performing well actually do perform better, often dramatically better.

At the risk of simplifying an extremely complex subject, there are two primary reasons why mental rehearsal improves performance levels.

The first is that your subconscious mind cannot distinguish between a real event and one that is vividly visualized. So if you see yourself hitting a ball with a bat beautifully in your mind, and you replay that vision repeatedly over several weeks, you will in all probability improve your standard of hitting because the subconscious believes you're practicing it for real.

The second reason visualization works so well was only discovered relatively recently. It has to do with your brain's plasticity.

When you have a thought or perform an action, a physical pathway in your brain is created, known as a synapse. If you repeat that thought or action, the pathway gets strengthened. So if you continually practice doing the same thing (even if it's only in your mind), as the pathway gets stronger you tend to get better at it. Your brain actually changes its structure to help you do that task more easily.

For example, there was a test where scientists got monkeys to push a button repeatedly over several days. The researchers discovered that certain paths (neural pathways) inside the monkeys' brains got stronger and thicker as they pushed the button. Then when they ceased making the monkeys press the button each day, the neural pathways got thinner and weaker again. It's this ability of the brain to adapt to changing circumstances that is known as neuroplasticity, and it's one of the most exciting fields of medicine today.

Its implications are profound. If mentally repeating something makes you better at it, you should be able to improve your performance in almost every area of your life simply by seeing yourself doing it well, repeatedly, in your mind.

In my own life, I have definitely found this to be the case. I am certainly far from perfect, but over the years I have visualized myself as being excellent in all kinds of life arenas and, sure enough, I've usually started to perform better in those fields.

So when I sit in my chair and see myself performing well in my mind's eye, I often get quite excited because I know that in a few days or weeks my results will begin to improve. Furthermore, just visualizing success puts me in a really good mood. It gets me focusing on solutions, not problems. It makes me more positive, more hopeful, more committed to taking the daily actions that I know will get me ahead in life.

Try it yourself for a week, 5 minutes each day. I assure you that soon you'll be feeling more confident about achieving your goals and definitely happier and more motivated.

AFFIRM YOUR SUCCESS

Next on my morning training list are affirmations. This is simply the technique of saying aloud words or phrases that help you focus on your goals and increase your belief in your ability to achieve them.

I usually say mine to myself for five minutes or so as I'm driving to the gym in the morning. Here are some of the phrases I say to myself three times each during my drive.

I am always happy and relaxed.   I am highly organized.
I am highly effective.   I am always grateful.
I exercise five times a week.   I uplift others.
I have great health and a great body.   I am a master of my mind.
I enjoy every day.   I am a champion.
I am clear and focused.   I love my work.

Right now many of you are probably laughing at such a technique, but before you scoff too much, you should know that some of the world's finest athletes use similar affirmations to maximize their performance.

Alex Rodriguez, one of the greatest baseball players of all time (and definitely one of the richest), is one of them. Rodriguez made history when he signed the world's first $250 million sports contract.

Here's what Alex had to say about his affirmation and visualization routine:

The way I use my mind is the biggest reason I've been able to enjoy success. I try to attain goals mentally first. Let me give you an example. I don't want to sound cocky, but early in the 1996 season, I visualized winning the American League Most Valuable Player award and holding it above my head. I visioned winning the batting title and holding up that trophy too . . . that year I missed winning the MVP by three votes and won the batting title.

Just as I believe in dreams, I believe in the power of positive reinforcement and visualization. Some nights when I go to bed I will tell myself, maybe 150 times, "I hit the ball solid. I hit the ball solid. What do I do for a living? I hit the ball solid" . . . I see the results from my mind's eye out . . . I believe a champion wins in his mind first, then he plays the game, not the other way around. It's powerful stuff.

These are not the words of a crazy man. These are the words of a person dedicated to performing at the absolute highest levels, a true champion. If you are serious about achieving at a world-class level, give affirmations a go for a couple of weeks—you'll be surprised at their powerful effect.

Right, let's just do a brief recap on where we are in the mental fitness regime. Each morning you are spending a few minutes visualizing perfect performance, and saying affirmations that focus you on your aims. Then throughout the day you are using the SCORE technique to remain clear and positive, and the Breath Release technique to let go of stress as it occurs.

The Daily Review

The final part of my daily mind maintenance system only takes about two minutes, and I do it just before I go to sleep.

It consists of two parts. The first is the Daily Performance Review. The DPR is incredibly easy—it's just a quick one-minute appraisal of my activities that day. I simply ask myself:

What did I do well?
What could I have done better?

It's a fantastic technique because so often we go to bed without ever really evaluating how our day went and how well we performed. But when we consciously review our daily actions, we usually see errors that can be fixed easily once we're aware of them. As top success coach Robin Sharma says, "Awareness precedes clarity. Clarity precedes results."

Schedule Your Gratitude

Finally we come to the Gratitude Minute. Here I simply spend 60 seconds or so thinking of all the good things that happened today and listing some of the things I should be grateful for in my life. You can list all kinds of stuff, from small things like a fun moment with a work colleague, a nice lunch, or a meeting that went well, to the bigger things in life, such as how lucky you are to live in the country you live in. I'll be grateful for my health, or that I have people around me that love me. There are so many things to be grateful for when you put your mind to thinking about them.

Once you get into the habit of doing the Gratitude Minute you'll never want to give it up, because it makes you feel really good inside. And when you start remembering those positive things every evening, you'll be pleasantly surprised at how many things happen in a single day that are amazing, fun, heartwarming, entertaining, or just plain positive. Yet without a regular reminder like the Gratitude Minute, we often never even notice them, or certainly don't appreciate them. Truly, the Gratitude Minute is one of the most uplifting exercises you can do for both your mind and your heart.

A SYSTEM THAT WORKS

So that's the system I use to prevent destructive thinking, and it really works for me. Try it and I bet you'll find it works for you, too. Don't get psyched out by all the different techniques I'm suggesting you do each day. Trust me—it's really easy once you get used to it. Your daily mind makeover can take as little as 16 minutes a day:

Morning visualization: 5 minutes
Morning affirmations: 5 minutes
5 × SCORE routine: 2 minutes
5 × Breath Release: 2 minutes
Evening review: 1 minute
Evening gratitude: 1 minute

And what an important 16 minutes! This daily ritual will make you happier, more focused, more committed, more relaxed, more appreciative, and more self-aware.

If you're a businessperson, you're likely to be sharper, more effective, more successful, and, eventually, wealthier. If you're a stay-at-home parent, this mind ritual will not only make you more optimistic and more efficient, but will also increase your fun levels.

If you're a student, you'll become much more motivated, less intimi-dated by obstacles, and a nicer person to be around. Everyone prefers the company of someone who's dynamic and positive, with the kind of warm, winning attitude that this program creates.

Your mind is your greatest weapon in the battle of life. Learn to use it better than your competition and you'll soon run rings around them. Do nothing to look after the state of your mind and the mental weeds will slowly grow and pull you down.

The Daily Mind Ritual has really helped me and I'm really excited at the thought of what it will do for you. Performed diligently, it will dramatically lift the quality of your entire life.

low productivity

Ever wonder how some people achieve colossal things in their lives? How some men and women hit goal after goal, while others waste entire years (or even decades) without getting anything major done?

I do. In fact, I've spent thousands of hours studying exactly that. And I've found that at the heart of most high achievers' lives is their highly effective use of time.

It makes sense when you think about it. Now more than at any other time in history, we are overloaded with tasks to complete. E-mail, the Internet, and mobile phones may have made communication easier, but they have also helped make life vastly more complex. More people want to reach us more often. They're ever more impatient, too. Expected response-rate times have been reduced by so much that many people get irritated if you don't reply to their e-mail within an hour. An hour!

No wonder we're so often stressed out—the pace of life has reached a ridiculous speed. It ain't gonna get any slower, either. Rather, it's virtually certain that the interruptions and stresses of work life will get ever more frequent. So we're left with just one choice: slip behind our competitors or learn to get more done, faster.

I've elected to do the latter.

FROM DISORGANIZED TO PRODUCTIVE

I was one of the most disorganized people I've ever known. When I was in my early twenties my bedroom was a mess, my car was full of rubbish and paraphernalia, and I would regularly lose all kinds of important stuff. At work I was not using my time well: I was doing unimportant jobs and not being at all focused.

I have to tell you it was incredibly frustrating and stressful at times to live like this. So one day I said, "Enough's enough!" and started to study the science of productivity and organization. Slowly but surely I discovered ways to get things done efficiently, to not procrastinate, and to achieve big things without overwhelming effort. It changed my life.

If you view yourself as chronically disorganized and feel you'll never be a high-productivity person, think again. You can change—you really can. I did.

These days I'm generally pretty good at staying organized, and it's largely because I focus on being productive every day. I've also found a whole plethora of productivity tools that help me immensely.

In the next few pages I want to share with you some of the best productivity tips I've gleaned from over twenty years of study of the subject. Put these techniques into daily use and I guarantee you will become significantly more productive.

PLAN BEFORE YOU START

Few people thoroughly plan what work they need to get done before they begin it. Our society praises people who are doing, doing, doing. There's a tremendous social pressure to be busy all the time. But you need to resist that with all your might and discipline yourself to pause for a while and plan before you start working your tail off.

This is ideally done three ways: planning what you want to achieve in the following year, planning what you need to get done in the next week, and, finally, planning your day.

For now, let's focus on the weekly and daily plans.

To create a weekly plan, it's best if you find about 15 minutes on a Friday afternoon or perhaps a Sunday (try to make it a habit by doing it at the same time each week).

Begin by thinking about the most important things you must get done in the next seven days. Not necessarily the most urgent, but the most important—the really high-value tasks. There will typically be between three and seven of these ultra-important jobs.

Then write these weekly key tasks on a piece of paper and put it where you can see it each day. Putting the weekly list where you'll constantly see it is a really effective way to keep you focused on what's important rather than getting caught up with the never-ending trivial tasks that life bombards you with.

Next comes your daily plan, one of the most valuable things you can do in your life.

Simply write down a list of no more than 10 tasks you should get done that day. You may like to group them into categories, for example, five work tasks, three social tasks, and two admin chores.

Then, simply apply the ABC method of prioritization. It's dead easy. If the task is really important and valuable, put an "A" next to it. If it's reasonably important but not absolutely vital, write a "B" next to it. Finally, if the job is relatively unimportant scribble a "C" next to it on your list.

Then discipline yourself to do the As first.

A simple plan, but hard to achieve! Life has a way of enticing us to do all those easy tasks on our to-do list—the ones that don't really matter—before we do the big ones. But using the ABC system makes it much more likely that you'll get the tasks that really count done first.

If you have a daily to-do list you'll be way ahead of most people when it comes to effectiveness. If you want to get even further ahead of the pack you need to add ABCs to it. It's an exceedingly powerful productivity technique used by some of the most effective people in the world.

CREATE BLOCKS OF TIME TO DO JOBS

The more you get interrupted, the less effective you'll be. Productivity expert Brian Tracy has said that it usually takes three times as long as the interruption itself to get over the interruption and back to full concentration again. To get loads of stuff done, you really must block out chunks of quiet time where you can work solidly without interruption for an extended period. Do this and your daily productivity will skyrocket.

There are several ways you can block out time to work. You can tell your colleagues not to interrupt you for one or two hours at a particular time each day. You can work at home or in a nearby café. Or you can book a boardroom or conference room in your office for an hour or two. Sure, it can sometimes be hard to lock yourself away, but you must insist that other people respect your quiet time. For the first few days people will barge in on you, but after a firm word or two from you they'll soon get the message.

Even at home this method works. The fact is, any task gets done more quickly and easily when you force yourself to stick to it without pausing or being interrupted. Try this technique and you'll enjoy a quantum leap in your effectiveness.

THINK 80/20

What a wonderful principle this is. The famous 80/20 rule was popularized by an Italian economist named Vilfredo Pareto in the 19th century. Basically it shows that in almost any area of life, about 80 percent of the results come from 20 percent of the actions.

The breakthrough that stems from this principle is clear: around 80 percent of what you do hardly matters at all! This is a provocative, even startling theory at first, but soon becomes an exciting one. Because if only 20 percent of what you do gets you most of the good results, you don't have to spend countless hours at work. All you have to do is concentrate on the very small, vital tasks that really make a difference.

This may seem elementary, but its ramifications are profound. When you start following the 80/20 rule all day long, it is absolutely amazing what you can get done. Very often just one simple hour's work spent on that crucial top 20 percent of tasks will make a massive impact on your results. Just imagine what you could achieve if you spent all day working on that important 20 percent—you could literally increase your productivity by a whopping 400 percent!

The 80/20 rule isn't just a revolution in effectiveness; it's a huge stress reliever too. Make 80/20 thinking a major part of your life and you won't feel as overloaded with unimportant work jobs, you'll be able to leave work earlier, you'll be promoted faster, get rich quicker and, if you like, retire earlier. All these delightful results will be possible because you'll be achieving significantly more with much less effort.

But living the 80/20 way is not easy. It's very tempting to be conventional in our use of time. It takes considerable courage to buck the usual work trends and work in different ways to everyone else.

Some of your coworkers won't like it. Some of your friends will find your new productivity habits peculiar, too. You yourself will find that you will regularly slip back into the traditional hard-slog ways of working. But stick with it. Make 80/20 thinking a habit and you'll be laughing all the way to the bank—not to mention enjoying a superior way of life with minimal stress and maximum achievement.

I believe in the 80/20 rule so strongly that I literally have those numbers framed on my desk where I can see them each and every day. Once it becomes part of your day it can make a stupendous difference to the quality of your life.

By the way, the most renowned expert on 80/20 theory is Richard Koch, a highly successful entrepreneur and venture capitalist who has written no less than three books just on this subject. My favourite is *Living the 80/20 Way* and I heartily recommend it.

RUSH UNIMPORTANT TASKS

This is the corollary of the last point. If most of what you do isn't really of great value, you should rush to finish it as soon as you can. Rushing the unimportant is a powerful method to free up large loads of time, giving you more to spend on the vital few activities that really count.

Now to be clear, I'm not suggesting you cut corners to such an extent that you do a half-complete, shoddy job—merely that you don't spend ages finessing your work unnecessarily. The truth is that good enough is often good enough, if the task isn't crucially important.

One way I rush unimportant tasks is to set a time limit on each job. For example, part of my daily to-do list might look like this:

Write article (15)
Call David (5)
Think about China Project (10)
Decide hotel (10)

You can see that after each task I put the maximum number of minutes I aim to spend on it. This keeps me from spending ages on jobs just because I've got time or they're easy and fun. Often I like to turn it into a game. I try to race myself, aiming to finish the job before my deadline is up. I find this technique not only makes me more productive, but it also gives me a burst of energy as I pick up the pace and get more committed to completing the task.

As the famous Parkinson's Law states, "Work expands so as to fill the time available for its completion." There is so much truth in that! Beware those little unimportant tasks. They will take control of your life if you let them. Do them fast and you will not only finish your to-do list earlier, you'll gain real momentum, feel more in control, and quickly get on top of your workload. Make the rushing technique a part of your life starting today, and you'll find this month will be one of your most productive ever.

DELEGATE WHAT ISN'T VITAL

Some people are addicted to working. But their very industriousness often keeps them from achieving very much because they can't resist doing every task themselves.

Delegation is the antidote to this obsession with doing everything. It can be tough to learn, but it's a crucial skill if you want to excel long term.

There are three levels of delegation, as I see it.

1. Delegate the Unimportant

First, delegate those tasks that aren't crucial or lucrative. If you're in business, the criterion for what's important is simple: does it make you money, or help you keep clients or staff? If not, flick it to someone else in your organization if you possibly can.

2. Delegate What You Are Not Good At

Let's face it: there are probably only four or five things (at most) that anyone is really excellent at. Many people have just one or two. Think about your own and take a minute to list them.

Once you've identified your areas of excellence, your job is to try to devote as much of your day as possible to doing those tasks. They are your areas of speciality. It sounds simple, but in practice it can be quite difficult. Many people understand this concept intellectually but still end up spending half their day doing stuff they're not good at—like bookkeeping, cleaning up around the office, administration, or tinkering with PowerPoint slides.

Stick with your strengths; they got you to where you are today. Focus on them, develop them, make them the best they can be—all of which you can only do if you devote most of your day to them.

3. Delegate What You Don't Enjoy Doing

Finally we come to the third area of delegation: delegate what you don't enjoy doing. Some people can't handle this one. They don't think enjoyment should come into the equation. To them, success is all about "no pain, no gain." I beg to differ. Spending time doing the things you enjoy is crucial to success, primarily because when you enjoy doing something you tend to do it better and for longer.

There's another important reason why maximizing your enjoyment is important. Life isn't just about money or achievement. Delegating as many unenjoyable things as you can is a valid strategy simply because it puts more fun in your life. After all, when you're on your deathbed you won't be thinking about the money you made. You'll be reminiscing about all the fun you had, whether at work or at play. Surely this counts at least as much as any point about productivity or time-effectiveness.

GETTING HELP

Those are the three main types of delegation, but as you read through them, some of you may be thinking that there's one small problem with my delegation strategy. You've got no one to delegate to! Maybe you're the junior in the company, you're a one-person office, or you're a parent at home on your own.

Well, when it comes to business I have firm views on this. If you can possibly afford it, you should have an assistant, even if it's only part-time. Someone to do all the trivia, all the admin, leaving you to do the important income-producing stuff. Now you may think you can't afford to hire an assistant—but I would argue that most people can't afford not to.

The average executive or business owner probably spends no more than two hours a day doing stuff that actually increases income. The rest of the day is spent doing paperwork, sitting in meetings, or churning through e-mails.

With a good assistant helping you, you can turn these highly productive two hours into four hours. So you can quite literally double the amount of time you spend making money. You should easily be able to make enough to afford the assistant. Think about it.

Why not start off hiring an assistant for a few hours a week, or for the mornings only? Then be disciplined with yourself and really focus on using the extra time you've freed up to generate more income. Try it. You'll find that having an assistant pays off fast.

For parents at home or people not working in business, having an assistant can be achieved in different ways. You could team up with other parents, friends, or associates and form a work group. Delegate tasks to each other, sharing the tough ones and trying to match jobs with people's natural likes and talents. There may well be jobs you don't like but other people don't mind, and vice versa. Plus, if one of you needs a day off, the others can carry the load.

Get good at this concept and you'll end up doing fewer of the things you don't enjoy and also have a strong support team around you. It's at least worth a try.

Split Your Time into 10-Minute Segments

I learnt this trick from the great entrepreneur Ingvar Kamprad, the founder of the mighty Swedish furniture retailer IKEA. Kamprad developed a unique technique for saving time and getting things done, helping him achieve more in a day than many folks do in a week. He discovered that when he separated his work day into 10-minute blocks, he was able to get a huge amount done. By working within such a short time line he found he boosted his momentum and increased his concentration.

As Kamprad put it, "Time is your important resource. You can do so much in 10 minutes. Ten minutes are not just one-sixth of your hourly pay. Ten minutes are a piece of yourself. Divide your life into 10-minute units and sacrifice as few of them as possible in meaningless activity."

It's a radical technique, but I love it. Not only does it increase your overall productivity, but it also helps you do stuff you're not looking forward to doing.

Say, for instance, you hate making new business cold calls. You may have been putting them off for weeks (or years!). This technique makes it easy. You just spend 10 minutes doing the calls. After all, anyone can do something for only 10 minutes. But as the saying goes, begun is half done. Once you do those calls for 10 minutes, they'll no longer scare you as much and you'll probably keep making calls for another half-hour. But the additional point is this: even if you stop making those new business calls after 10 minutes, you've still made progress—progress you probably would never have made had you not started with just those few minutes' work.

The other important aspect of the 10-Minute Technique is the energy lift it gives you. When you work in 10-minute blocks, you work fast. You polish off tasks quickly, and find yourself raring to move on to the next one. That in itself gives you a real sense of confidence as your momentum increases.

The 10-Minute Technique is one of my favourite strategies when I'm feeling down or when I'm just a bit lethargic and lazy. I may be motivated most of the day, but there are also plenty of times when I'm not particularly excited by the work ahead. Sometimes I'm just plain dreading it. At times like these, getting truly engaged in work is difficult—often really difficult—but Kamprad's 10-Minute Technique helps me jump off the launch pad and right into whatever I've got on my to-do list.

The other reason I like the Kamprad time-management method is because I'm a real fan of what the guy has achieved. Not only has he built the biggest furniture store chain on the planet, he's made high-quality stylish furniture available to the masses and served as a role model with his humility, frugality, and modesty. Whenever I can, I try to learn from great people, and frankly if the 10-Minute Technique is good enough for a titan like Ingvar Kamprad, then it's certainly good enough for me.

The 2-Minute Rule

This is a tip from David Allen, a productivity expert I really admire. When going through your e-mails, in-tray, or to-do list, if you come across something you can resolve in two minutes or under, do it immediately.

Often we let things pile up until we have an intimidating mountain of tasks. The result? We are so overwhelmed by the magnitude of the tasks we have to do that we procrastinate about even starting on them. But with the 2-Minute Rule you regularly reduce your job list throughout the day, keeping it shorter and manageable.

It's good for you psychologically, too. By doing the quick jobs as they occur, you get a feeling of progress, a sense that you're on top of things. It's also quite amazing what you can do in under two minutes. Sometimes your day's most valuable achievements are done in virtually no time at all.

Isn't it true that you have numerous things you've wanted to do for months but somehow never got around to them? Give each of them two minutes' work. Time and time again you'll discover you can make genuine progress in that short time frame. Let's face it: half the battle of achievement is just doing something, anything, to move things forward.

So next time you're faced with a gargantuan wave of stuff to do, swiftly search through the tasks you can knock off in two minutes or less. You'll feel great after you've done them, and the people around you will be surprised at how speedily you seem to react to their requests and get done what needs to be done. Doing a few tasks quickly will often give you more leeway with your boss or clients to spend more time on other stuff. When people see that you're delivering the goods in some areas they're likely to be lenient with you on others.

Play Baroque Music

Have I lost my mind? What has 350-year-old music got to do with being more productive?

As it turns out, plenty. Listening to baroque music while you work has been scientifically proven to increase your concentration, lift your creativity, and make you perform better.

How can this be possible? It's all to do with the beat of the music. Most baroque music follows a 4/4-time beat, which has been proven to relax the mind and improve synaptic connections in the brain. The result is significantly clearer thinking and enhanced brain functioning.

It's easy to test it for yourself. Just buy some Bach CDs or download some baroque orchestral tracks and play them while you work. It may take a few plays to get used to the sound, but pretty soon you'll be working with more energy and efficiency.

Right near my desk I keep an MP3 player. Each morning when I get to work I put on some baroque music and keep it on for around half an hour. Like most people, I can feel a bit sluggish some mornings, but once that music is on I soon feel better and sharper.

Incidentally, just as baroque music helps you think, listening to a lot of heavy-metal music can actually reduce your brain's effective functioning. The brain craves stimulation—but not too much. Even if you don't want to use baroque music, you need to find music that has real energy and verve but that is still relaxing.

Use a Negative Ion Generator

The brain is only 3 percent of the body's weight, yet it uses around 20 percent of the body's total oxygen intake. That makes it pretty clear that oxygen is a vital component of the brain's smooth operation. So it makes sense that the purer and cleaner the oxygen you breathe is, the better you'll work.

But in today's cities breathing pure air is almost impossible. Pollution, electrical fields, grit, and grime are the norm in most metropolises and they greatly reduce the air quality and therefore the quality of your thinking.

It's just like petrol for a car. Fill your tank with low-quality, dirty fuel and obviously your vehicle won't perform at its peak. Put the finest fuel in and you can drive faster for longer. Same with your brain. It thrives on clean oxygen and is lethargic without it.

It's all got to do with the ions in the air. Out in the countryside the air has about 50 percent positive ions and 50 percent negative ions. But in the city the balance gets out of whack. Often you'll find three times more positive ions than negative ions, which means poor-quality fuel for the brain.

So if you want your mind to perform at peak levels, either live in the country or use a machine that rebalances the air, such as a negative ion generator.

You can find negative ion generators at most major department stores, and they're simple to use. You just plug them in and they immediately start purifying the air around you. (I have two, one near my desk at work and one in my bedroom. That way I get six or seven hours of ultra-pure air every night as I sleep.)

It may seem a little unusual at first to have such machines in your life, but if you want to perform at your best you must always be looking at tools that can assist you. A good negative ion generator is proven technology that can do exactly that.

Become a Master of Life Productivity

There you have it. A whole stack of methods and techniques you can use each day to maximize your productivity. (To get even more productivity tips, visit www.whypeoplefail.org.)

Make no mistake—these procedures work. I know, because I use them all myself. If they can help someone as disorganized as I once was to become efficient, they can do the same for you.

On the other hand, if you don't become a master at time management and life productivity, then you have only one alternative if you seek to excel. And that is to work longer hours than your competition—a tactic that is ultimately both exhausting and boring.

But become a great time manager and you can quite literally achieve more in a day than some people achieve in a week. And more in a year than most achieve in a decade.

fixed mindset

Imagine if there was a way of thinking that almost guaranteed that you would become a success in life, a belief system that the vast majority of "geniuses" shared and most average performers didn't.

Imagine if this attitude was learnable and that when you adopted it, almost every area of your life would improve.

Well, in the view of the eminent professor of psychology Carol Dweck, there is such a way of thinking. It's called the Growth Mindset.

Dweck and her students have spent the last twenty years researching whether the mindset you have affects whether you will fail or succeed in life. Their results are remarkable and potentially life-changing.

Professor Dweck had long known that our beliefs affected our performance in all manner of ways, but over time she discovered that there are two mindsets that govern a human's failure rate most powerfully: the Fixed Mindset and the Growth Mindset.

Let's take a look at the features of each one, then delve into the ramifications stemming from each particular mode of thinking.

FIXED MINDSET

People with a fixed mindset believe that their qualities and abilities are set in stone. They think they have been given a fixed amount of intelligence and a certain set of talents and basically that's that. For the rest of their lives they must work within these given talents and abilities and not try to go beyond them. In their mind there is no way they can improve on what they've been born with.

Now according to Dweck's research, if you have this mindset then all sorts of consequences ensue.

For a start, you won't like to reveal your limitations to other people. People with a fixed mindset prefer to keep secret any areas in which they don't excel. That really makes sense when you think about it. If I believe I only have a certain level of intelligence, then I will probably want to avoid revealing my intellectual limits to others. However, this mindset leads to all sorts of negative behavior throughout life, such as:

Not trying hard. Dweck's research has shown that people with a fixed mindset don't usually try really hard on a tough challenge. Why? Simply because they might fail and look bad. They feel that if they try hard and fail, then other people will see that they have limitations. But if they don't try too hard at things, they have a ready-made excuse if they fail—they were just playing around, not giving it their all. They also believe that their talent is all they need to succeed, so there's not much reason to try hard anyway. (You can imagine how much this attitude limits their success in life.)

Giving up early. People with a fixed mindset like to give the impression that life is effortless for them. They believe that through their pure talent they should be able to achieve great things. Therefore, when faced with trying something really challenging they will often shy away from persisting with it so as not to risk revealing their limitations. If they're not making quick progress on a goal, they often give up rather than risk looking bad to other people around them, and they then feel bad about themselves inside.

Not expanding their expertise. Usually those burdened with a fixed mindset feel the need to show that they are intelligent or have great talent. The tricky part for them, however, is that because they don't like trying new fields (because they may not be immediately good at them) they are forced to show their talents only in those areas that they're already very confident in. So they keep doing the same things they excel at and rarely widen their skill base into new areas. So you can see that just by taking on this way of thinking, life is likely to become pretty limiting. Fixed mindsetters are stuck in a pretty small world. They don't expand their world because they don't like the uncomfortable feeling of not being good at something. They prefer to stick with what they know they're competent at, even if many opportunities are lost as a result.

Now let's take a look at the growth mindset personality—what it is and the characteristics of people who possess it.

GROWTH MINDSET

People with a growth mindset believe that talents are not fixed. They think that even if you're not good at something at first, you can become good at it eventually through dedicated and consistent effort.

The world of growth mindsetters centers around learning—basically they believe that learning is the secret to success in any field and happiness in life. In fact, there's nothing they enjoy more than learning and growing their skills.

They believe passionately that their abilities are not fixed. They feel that anything you can do, they can do too—with enough practice and time.

The person with a growth mindset finds it tremendously stimulating to stretch themselves beyond their current capacities. Bob Dylan's famous quote "If you're not growing you're dying" could easily be the growth mindsetter's motto.

It's an exciting way of thinking because it leads to some dynamic and fulfilling ways of behavior, including:

Not giving up easily. Typical growth-mindset individuals are highly persistent. That's because they don't mind getting things wrong at first. They enjoy the process of solving the difficulties put in front of them; in fact, they often seek out difficult things. They get a thrill confronting a challenge and trying their utmost to conquer it. Tough battles rarely dishearten them, and actually often invigorate them.

Optimistic thinking. Growth mindsetters aren't just pie-in-the-sky Pollyannas; they have their down moods like anyone else. But because they believe they can learn to overcome their setbacks, they tend to be much more positive about life than the fixed-mindset people around them. This general optimism leads to less stress, more happiness, and improved effectiveness. Setbacks seem merely temporary to growth-mindset people, as they usually remain optimistic and upbeat about their lives.

Fast improvement: It's easy to see that folks with a growth mindset will continue to improve in just about any area they focus on. It's virtually inevitable that life gets better for growth mindsetters, if for no other reason than that they are continually working on improving the situations around them. They may have less intelligence and less talent than a fixed mindsetter, but because they're always growing and getting better they eventually surpass the fixed mindsetter. Long term, a less "intelligent" growth-mindset person will often achieve much more than their high-IQ, fixed-mindset competitors, simply because they keep refining their abilities until they become excellent.

You may be familiar with the Japanese concept of kaizen. It's a philosophy that has been central to Japanese manufacturing for over fifty years and played a crucial role in the rise of Japan's industrial power after World War II. The English translation for kaizen is "small and continuous improvements." The Japanese believe that if the spirit of kaizen is applied to any area with regularity, that area is sure to get better.

People with a growth mindset are masters of kaizen. They are always looking at ways to improve their skills, talents, and abilities, even if just a little bit. Eventually that commitment to incremental improvement leads to enormous gains and massive improvements in life satisfaction. Inch by inch, little by little, every aspect of their lives gets better.

At the heart of growth-mindset people's effectiveness is how well they handle failure. Those with a growth mindset are not immune to pain, even depression at times, but because they believe they can learn to find a solution to any problem, they persevere and eventually often conquer. No situation is hopeless to the growth mindsetter. They are confident they can overcome hardship—they just need to learn how.

YOU CAN LEARN ANYTHING

One of the great myths of life that many failures believe is true is that some people are just born superior. Although there are clearly some genetic differences in intelligence, the truth is that your awesome brain is so powerful that it can learn to overcome virtually any disadvantage you are born with (as long as you are basically of sound mind).

What Dweck showed in her studies is that many of the greats of history were not actually born geniuses. They developed their startling abilities through monumental ambition and plain old hard practice. They worked for their greatness.

Thomas Edison may have been the most outstanding inventor of all time, but it was his awesome appetite for long working hours that really made the difference. It is said he worked until so late in the night that he regularly slept in his lab. According to folklore, it took him over 10,000 unsuccessful experiments before he created his first incandescent light bulb, thus changing the world forever. Without his staggering amount of grueling effort Edison may have been just an ordinary, mediocre achiever.

As he himself said, when asked what was the secret to success, it is "the ability to apply your physical and mental abilities to one problem incessantly without growing weary." Or to put it more plainly: work really, really, really, really hard.

We may marvel at Mozart's "natural-born genius," but few people know that he had been writing music for 10 years before he composed any of his famous pieces. Yes, 10 years of hard slog preceded his greatness, as it does for almost anyone who achieves something substantial.

Michael Jordan may be celebrated as perhaps the finest basketball player of all time, but he didn't even make the top team at his high school. Then, even when he was at the top of the NBL it was well known that he would usually arrive earlier to practice and stay later than his teammates. Jordan knew that even with his so-called "talent," the secret to his lasting success was always going to be hard work.

Albert Einstein was viewed as mediocre by his schoolteacher, yet he rose to the top through sheer dedication and drive.

This dedication to practice and slow improvement was shown in researcher Benjamin Bloom's study on super-achievers. Bloom looked at the early lives of 120 super-performers in a wide variety of fields: tennis players, swimmers, doctors, scientists, concert pianists, and so on.

He found a very surprising thing. The majority of the superstars did not show unusual powers or talents as kids, nor in their early teens. Looking at them as 10- or 11-year-olds you would find it hard to set them apart talent-wise from other kids in their neighborhood. What made the difference was consistent motivation and effort and a good strong support network around them.

This, of course, is fantastically good news for the rest of us. It means that if we just focus on developing a growth mindset, the sky really is the limit.

GROWTH-MINDSET LEADERS

A growth mindset is not just applicable to your own life; it's very relevant to how you can affect the lives of others, too. When you look at the most effective leadership styles, you see again and again that it's leaders with a growth mindset who inspire high performance, loyalty, and long-term commitment from those following them. Professor Dweck's research shows that in business, growth-mindset managers have specific traits that help them lead.

Firstly, they are nurturers. Not for them the hierarchical, domination style of leadership, no siree. These leaders are all about looking for, encouraging, and praising the efforts of their staff, even if those efforts fail to yield the results required. By nurturing and inspiring their employees to try their hardest almost regardless of the result, such leaders often change the whole culture of their company. Their staff become more hopeful, more optimistic about themselves and their company. As a result they become more passionate about their work, which soon leads to better and better results for the company.

Employees feel that it is permissible to fail. In fact, the best growth-mindset leaders applaud failure—if it yields valuable lessons or if those who have failed tried their hardest.

There's a famous story about the great former general manager and CEO of IBM, Thomas Watson. An employee had made a serious mistake and was summoned to Watson's office. Certain he was about to be fired, the employee sheepishly entered the business titan's office, his head held low.

"I suppose this means I'm out of a job, Mr. Watson," the employee dejectedly remarked.

"Are you kidding?" responded Watson. "It cost me almost a million dollars to teach you this lesson—why would I want to get rid of you now that you've learned it?"

As you can imagine, the staff member left the CEO's office uplifted and inspired.

The man many believe was the greatest large-corporation CEO that America has ever produced, Jack Welch, had a similar experience when he was just a lowly manager at General Electric.

Welch approved an experiment that led to a massive explosion in the factory he was in charge of. Although nobody was hurt, it was a disaster of epic proportions.

That night Welch made the long, lonely drive to visit his boss's home and tell him the awful news. But the meeting did not go as he expected. Rather than get furious, this top executive peppered Welch with questions about what he was up to, what had happened and what he had learned from it. Welch walked out of the meeting with a new confidence that maybe he could make it in the company after all. This was growth-mindset leadership in action.

As a result of this experience, Welch himself began to cultivate a leadership style that uplifted and encouraged rather than belittled, demeaned, and dominated like that of so many other corporate chieftains.

Now that doesn't mean Welch was a weak leader. Quite the opposite. He became legendary for being one of the world's toughest managers on performance (incredibly, he advocated sacking the bottom 10 percent of his managers every year). But he also had the learning mindset firmly embedded in himself. He was his staff's cheerleader, coach, and (for the senior managers) mentor all rolled into one.

Welch had incredibly high standards, but he inspired his managers to rise to them, to ask more of themselves than they ever had before. As a consequence, their performance blossomed.

Another classic example of a growth-mindset leader is New York City's mayor, Michael Bloomberg. Consider this: Bloomberg was actually sacked from financial powerhouse Salomon Brothers, but rather than mope around feeling defeated he conceived a new kind of computer system for traders. He soon opened up for business and his new trading device caught on like wildfire. His business took enormous market share from arch-rival Reuters and eventually made Bloomberg a multibillionaire.

Many people in their late fifties who have achieved so much would probably rest on their victory laurels. Not Bloomberg. As a true growth mindsetter he looked for a new challenge. He decided that he would walk away from running his giant multinational organization and try to become mayor of New York.

As we know, remarkably he achieved this aim, but even then he proceeded to play out some classic growth-mindset maneuvers. First, he dispensed with the grand mayoral office and took an open-plan cubicle right among his staff. Second, he sat humbly with the heads of various city departments and open-mindedly listened to their complaints, ideas, and visions for a better New York.

Many people also believe that Bloomberg may one day even make a run to become the president of the United States. Why not? To a true growth-mindset-oriented person, any skill can be learned, any opportunity mastered if they work hard, long, and diligently. I take my hat off to Michael Bloomberg for his courage, vision, and self-belief. What an inspiration!

THE RESULTS ARE CLEAR

No matter what area of life you study, the two mindsets are clearly seen. And in every area researched, those people with a growth mindset achieve better results and more happiness than those with a fixed mindset.

Take personal relationships as an example. There are millions of people who hold the view that their (or their partner's) behavior traits are permanent and impossible to change. "That's just the way I am," they lament. But this is often not the case. Human beings are highly malleable—they can adjust, adapt, and dramatically change if they are encouraged and motivated to do so.

But it takes work, and hard work is not the fixed-mindset person's view of what a relationship should be. They believe that if you have to work at a relationship then maybe it wasn't meant to be. They want the fairytale, the riding off into the sunset, happily ever after. If it doesn't turn out like that, they think there's something wrong and usually unfixable— with themselves, their partner, or the "chemistry" of their relationship.

Growth mindsetters, however, might start out all romantic, looking for their Prince or Princess Charming, but they don't expect a totally smooth ride. They know that even a successful relationship will take hard work at times and that differences can be worked out. And they're prepared to do the work to make their relationship the best it can be.

OVERCOMING CHALLENGES

They also believe that just because there's a challenge in the relationship, it doesn't mean that either person is actually flawed as a human being. The problem with that way of thinking, of course, is that if you believe your partner's character is flawed in some way, then there's nothing you can really do about it. It's fixed (just like the mindset of someone who thinks this way). When either person in a relationship takes on this point of view, it's just a matter of time before the union begins to unravel.

Those with a growth mindset don't shy away from problems (in fact, they're more likely to address them) but they don't blame, either. They understand that there may be a problem with the situation, but not necessarily with the person. They know that nobody's perfect, even the ideal partner—that there is no relationship without its share of challenges. They acknowledge each person's limitations, then start work on overcoming them. What a recipe for success.

Even when a relationship breaks up, the way that growth-mindset people think remains useful. This shows in several key ways. After a break-up, those with a growth mindset tend to:

Forgive more. They don't necessarily forgive to the point of wanting to take their partner back (quite the opposite, often), but they also usually don't harbor anger, resentment, and bitterness towards their ex long term. Their view is typically that the relationship may have been a bad idea, but they're going to try to let it go and move on. That kind of attitude may not reduce the emotional pain of the break-up, but it's likely to reduce how long the pain ultimately lasts.

See their misery as not permanent. This is important. Even in the midst of the most grueling emotional pain, the growth mindsetter knows deep down that this too shall pass. And precisely because they can see that there is a light at the end of the relationship tunnel, they continue their lives with at least some optimism and hope. At times this thin but strong thread of positivity that runs through their lives can be life-saving.

Try to learn from it. Maybe not in the heat of the breakup, but in the following weeks and months after their relationship meltdown, growth-mindset people look deep into themselves. They ask themselves, "How could I have prevented this? How should I change for my next relationship? In what ways can I improve how I behave?" These questions are hard to address and often even harder to answer, but the result of such positive soul-searching is usually a richer, happier future life.

Look to the future. They may be emotionally fragile and they're definitely battle-weary, but once the relationship breakup dust has settled, those with a growth mindset start focusing on the future. Slowly but surely, they pick themselves up and begin re-creating their lives, searching again for a partner who is really right for them. They believe in the promise of a great future relationship because deep down they believe in themselves. They have faith in their ability to grow, adapt, and overcome any difficulties that may arise.

It's easy to see that if you have any one of these four beliefs, let alone all of them, you will be likely to thrive and recover more quickly after a relationship ends. Actually, these beliefs will help you get through any adversity.

So that's the power of the growth mindset in relationships, business, and life. In a nutshell, those with a growth mindset tend to succeed more and enjoy more, while those with a fixed mindset encage themselves in a smaller, poorer-quality world. Knowing this, no sane person would choose to have a fixed mindset.

CHANGING FOR GOOD

Many people reading this chapter may be wondering whether they can change their mindset from fixed to growth.

Well, the good news is that of course you can change, but like most things worth achieving it will take focus, effort, and time. In fact, you've already got one of the biggest parts of change handled: you now know that these two mindsets exist. Being conscious of these two ways of thinking is often enough to change behavior all by itself, according to Professor Dweck.

The next task if you want become a true growth mindsetter is to look at your life and make some plans. Ask yourself:

In what way would I like to improve?
How would I like to grow and change?
What would the "new me" look like? Feel like? Act like? Achieve?

These are exciting questions that can really get you moving forward in an empowered, dynamic way. Once you get clear on the directions you would like to grow in, write down a few steps you can take over the next few weeks to help get you there. Remember: you don't need to know *every* step along your growth road—just the next step. Once you've taken that step, the others will become clearer.

You'll be amazed at how designing a plan for growth and thinking about it just a little each day will transform your life. Once you focus on such a plan, all sorts of ways to fulfill it will pop into your mind.

Then as you encounter the inevitable obstacles in life, train yourself to always ask, "What can I learn from this? How can I use this to become a better person? What's the next step forward to improve the situation?"

These are simple questions, but when they are asked regularly they lead to rapid life improvement and turnaround.

A LIFE-CHANGING CONCEPT

I must say that learning about the power of the growth mindset has had a substantial impact on the quality of my own life. Now that I understand that constantly learning and growing is one of the key secrets to a high-quality life, I have accelerated my emphasis on studying new fields. More than ever, I'm seeking to expand my knowledge in my work and personal life.

Once you've reached a certain level of competency in a field, it's easy to coast along, performing a little above average and getting moderate rewards. But when you become excited about the power of continuous learning, things change fast. You put a little more pressure on your learning curve, you delve deeper into the area you're involved in, you push yourself a little closer to the outer edge of competence. Increased growth, progress, and satisfaction are the results.

Dweck's research has also made me think more about what my own actual talents are. There are many things I always just assumed I was no good at—math and finance are a couple that spring to mind. I remember getting shockingly low marks at school for math and dropping the subject the moment I could. I always just assumed that I was a numerical klutz and absolutely nothing could be done about it. The mindset research, however, caused me to question this belief.

When I look back on my days struggling with math in the classroom, I realize that the main reason I didn't excel at it was not because there was something inherently wrong with my brain. I wasn't missing some mysterious math gene. The simple truth was that I was bad at math because I never worked at being good at it. As soon as it got a bit difficult I gave up on it and slipped further and further behind. Clearly I had a negative, fixed mindset about it.

Knowing what I know now about growth mindset, I should have assumed that childhood math is very learnable and created a schedule for doing exactly that. No doubt once I concentrated on that area it would have gotten stronger. I may never have won a medal in the World Math Olympiad, but I wouldn't have sucked at it either.

So what areas of life have you just decided that you are no good at? Is it possible that the only reason you're not exceptional at them is because you haven't worked hard at becoming so? What would life be like if you were excellent in that area? Is it worth trying again?

These are powerful questions. When I think of what my life could become if I continuously focused on learning more, growing more, and becoming more, I get really excited.

Clearly the future for anyone with a growth mindset is huge.

weak energy

Here's the truth: success is a struggle.

Yes, there may be people who have found succeeding in life a cinch, but there are very few of them. Furthermore, once you read a few biographies of the rich, famous, and superbly talented you find good old-fashioned hard work was usually the factor that made the big difference. At times exhausting work. Tedious work. Stressful work.

Plenty of people start off on the road to success full of energy and drive, but because it's a long, long road to get to Fantastictown, they often run out of energy along the way. These folks are instantly recognizable walking down the street. Shoulders hunched over, eyes down, slowly shuffling along, they've lost their spark and drive.

Energy really is important to success. You need energy to work long hours, to think clearly, to remain positive. Yet very few people work on keeping their energy levels strong and powerful.

In our lifetime this will change, in my opinion. Entrepreneurs, top executives, even parents at home will start taking their energy levels more seriously, and try to maximize the energy they can create and maintain.

Low energy is a very big reason that people don't succeed. So many people would like to work harder and aim higher in life, but they've become weary from life's setbacks. Soon they forget their dreams and instead start focusing on just getting through the day, merely surviving rather than thriving.

If that sounds a bit like you, take heart, because in this chapter I'm going to present to you some sure-fire ways to get your energy powering, no matter what age you are. Boost your energy, and travelling down the success highway will become a whole lot easier, believe me.

Let's investigate some of these proven energy enhancers.

GOOD-QUALITY SLEEP IS CRUCIAL

The first way to increase your energy is to start monitoring your sleep patterns. Good-quality sleep is absolutely vital for high performance. When you sleep, your body's repair mechanisms go into overdrive. Your muscles are regenerated, your energy meridians are rejuvenated, your mind is replenished and reinvigorated.

There's also evidence that a shortage of sleep has been linked to blood pressure and cholesterol problems. A paucity of sleep may even be linked to cancer. Certainly late-night shift workers have a higher incidence of colon and breast cancer than those who work 9 to 5.

Getting lots of sleep may also help you lose weight. Two hormones, ghrelin and leptin, which help suppress appetite, are less plentiful if you don't sleep much. So it really is absolutely crucial that you get regular, high-grade sleep.

Here are a few areas you should take a look at to see if they might be affecting how well you sleep.

Darkness

Absolute darkness is crucial for high-quality snoozing. Your pineal gland is a vitally important brain regulator and very sensitive to light. Keep your room dark and your pineal gland tells your brain it's night-time and gets to work, helping your body to regulate your hormones and clean up your mental filing systems. Leave any light on and your brain's repair mechanisms will not work as strongly (kids should not have night lights for this reason). Get blinds or curtains that block out street lights completely.

Low Electrical Fields

Check to ensure you don't have electricity pulsing right near your body. Move electric clocks, heaters, TVs and sound systems well away from you if they're on—the electrical fields generated by this equipment can adversely affect your body's electric field, thereby making it less easy to relax and get to sleep. Ideally you should not have wires running underneath the bed either. Replace electric blankets with natural ones. Ideally, put your alarm clock in the next room. Not only will that help you sleep, having to get out of bed to turn it off will keep you from sleeping in.

Remove Dust

Remember, you'll often be in your bedroom for eight hours or more per day. The quality of the oxygen you breathe during that time will have a huge impact on the energy you have the next day. Regularly vacuum your bedroom and remove dust from furniture at least weekly, and your lungs will be less likely to fill with airborne impurities. Regular dusting and vacuuming also lessens the number of microscopic bugs that can inhabit your mattress and carpet. Your bedroom may look clean, but you would be stunned by how many tiny organisms actually live in it. Dusting and cleaning weekly won't just help you sleep—it could aid your overall health as well.

One of the best ways to clean your air of dust is to buy a negative ion generator. The generator exudes millions of negative ions that attach themselves to dust particles and help bring them to the floor of your bedroom. You can then vacuum them up. The air you breathe when you sleep should be treated very seriously. You spend around a third of your life in your bedroom—if you have low-quality air in there you'll have a lower-quality life.

Get at Least Seven Hours' Sleep

There are lots of theories about the right amount of sleep time. Many sleep experts say eight or nine hours. Some say at least seven. All I know is that it's pretty darn hard to live a rich work life and a fun social life and still get eight hours' sleep a night. If you can do it, good luck to you—I'm impressed. But if you're as busy as I am, you may have to settle for seven.

My advice is to not let yourself get less than seven hours' snoozing, no matter how busy you are. You may think it's a waste of time, but sleep has been shown to be crucial to your memory, your creativity, your mood, your speed of biological aging and, of course, your energy levels. Don't risk multilevel health damage; get a minimum of seven hours' rest a night. If you don't have time to get at least seven hours, then review your time-management systems—they are likely to be suboptimal.

EXAMINE YOUR DIET

What you eat dramatically affects your energy levels. For example, you will generally have more energy if you eat less meat. I know the thought of eating mostly whole grains, fruits, and vegetables is sacrilege to many people, but hear me out on this one. I've got a question for you: what two activities do you think use the most energy? The surprising answer is sex and food digestion. So if you consume lots of heavy meat meals, your body will use up lots of energy just breaking them down. In contrast, fruits and vegetables (which consist mostly of water) are really easy to digest, using a fraction of your body's energy. Try it for yourself over the next week and feel the energy difference.

Reduce your meat intake by half and you'll find you have considerably more energy each day. Isn't it true that when you have a big meat meal you often feel sluggish and even sleepy afterwards? Trying to digest meat is tiring and energy draining. Keep your meat intake low and your energy levels will soon rise.

By the way, there's another aspect of eating that directly affects your energy levels: how you chew your food. Gulp your spaghetti Bolognese down quickly and it means your stomach has to work much harder to digest it. Chew it well before you swallow and it's much easier for your stomach to process. Also, the more you chew, the more digestive juices are released by your stomach. Chewing well really is one of the secrets to maximizing your food's goodness.

IMPROVE YOUR ENVIRONMENT

The next area of energy enhancement concerns your mental energy: it's keeping your home and office tidy. You may not have connected a messy office to energy depletion, but the reality is that a messy environment is stressful. You lose stuff, you don't feel as good about yourself, you're sometimes not even sure what tasks you have to do when your place is in disarray. A messy environment is a major energy drainer.

There are two simple solutions to the mess problem. The first is to do a 10-minute clean every night as soon as you get home, or every morning before you head out for the day. It's important you do this at the same time each day so it becomes a habit (to help remind you, stick a Post-it up with the words "10-minute clean" where you can see it as soon as you come home).

The other elementary technique is to set aside time in your diary for a once-a-week 30-minute tidy-up. Good times to do this are Monday night or on the weekend. The trick, once again, is to schedule it in your diary so that it happens.

Believe me, once your work and home environments are neat and organized, a huge amount of psychic energy will be released. You'll have less to worry about and much more ordered thinking. After all, the state of your mind often mirrors the state of your surroundings.

EXERCISE

It's a huge energy booster. Now clearly this is not a physical fitness book, but it is a mental fitness book and there's a huge correlation between a healthy body and a mind filled with positive energy.

So many businesspeople claim to be dedicated to elite performance but do little or no exercise. That's crazy. When you exercise at least three times a week your energy goes through the roof. You think better, you can concentrate for longer and you're more optimistic to boot. In the future I believe almost all ambitious people will regularly exercise, simply because the benefits to performance are just too numerous to ignore.

If the thought of slipping on your sneakers makes you shudder, I've got a simple technique to help you out. Just go for a 10-minute walk every morning. Ten minutes is nothing. Anyone can do 10 minutes. But you just watch what happens. Even with just 10 minutes' exercise a day your blood flow will improve, your lungs will get more oxygen, your whole body (and your mind) will feel so much better for it. Then a funny thing will happen: you'll find it effortless to move to 15 minutes, then 20, then 30 or more. Pretty soon exercise will become a natural part of your life.

On the other hand, if you do not do any exercise, you are just kidding yourself if you think you are making the most of your energy potential. You'll be stuck in first gear. So take my seven-day Energy Challenge. Get up a little earlier and do just one week of 10-minute morning walks. It may seem to be too small an effort to be useful, but I assure you you'll find it makes a tangible difference.

STRETCH

The science of yoga has been around for over three thousand years. Beginning in India, then slowly spreading across Asia and the world over centuries, yoga is a deep, profound, highly organized system designed to unlock the higher levels of the body, mind, and soul.

You don't have to aspire to be a guru on a Himalayan mountaintop to get the benefits of yoga. Just five minutes a day of yoga stretching will help lift your energy enormously.

Here's why. According to yoga experts the body is an intricate but powerful energy power station. Lines of energy (known as meridians) are everywhere throughout your body, giving you the power to move, think, and breathe. But sometimes when you don't move much or you get stressed, the lines of energy get blocked. At first you'll hardly notice an energy blockage. But after a few weeks, you'll feel more lethargic and often a little depressed. That's where yoga stretching really helps. By simply doing a five-minute routine of 5–10 different stretches, you will open up these energy channels and get the energy flow moving again.

Serious yoga students think nothing of doing hours of yoga a day, but I'm guessing you don't have the time or inclination to go down that path. You'll be surprised what just five minutes of stretching can do for your energy levels. Half an hour after performing a basic series of yoga postures you'll feel more positive, more alive and more clear-headed. You'll move more easily, too, and be significantly more relaxed.

Conversely, if you don't stretch daily you'll have more bodily tension, feel more stressed, and get irritated more easily. Your energy levels will also be significantly lower. Yoga stretching is an almost miraculous body and mind enhancer.

There's no need for me to include a series of yoga positions in this book. Just search the term "yoga poses" on the Internet and pick 5–10 exercises that appeal to you. If you really get into the whole yoga lifestyle, the next step is to sign up for yoga classes; there are plenty around.

GET DAILY SUNLIGHT

The human body needs sunlight. When you go outside, sunlight enters through your eyes and skin and its energy is dispersed throughout your body. Experts have shown that ultraviolet rays help the mind function better, lift the mood and give the body vitamins D and E.

Sunlight also really lifts your energy. Actually, one of the main reasons I drive a convertible car is to increase the daily sunlight I receive. Being stuck in an office building all day sitting under neon lights doesn't exactly enhance your health. A few minutes out in the fresh air and sunshine rebalances the body and rejuvenates your energy levels.

Now there are some people who believe any sunlight is bad for you, that it causes cancer and ages you quickly. I think it's all a matter of degree. Most researchers in this area agree that a little daily sunlight is much better for you than no sunlight at all. A few hours a day, however, are likely to take a toll on your health over time.

If you're like most people who live in the city, it's more likely that you are not getting enough sunlight than that you are getting too much.

REGULATE YOUR LIFESTYLE

Take a look up at the sky this evening. You'll see a stunningly elaborate series of stars and planets moving like clockwork across the night sky. The universe is so ordered and organized that when a comet zooms past Earth, astronomers can tell us the exact time it will return to our planet, even if that time is centuries in the future!

As we are part of this great universe, I believe it's natural for us to live an ordered, organized life too. I'm not suggesting that we not be spontaneous and free in our lives, only that we need to support that freedom with strong daily systems of order and regularity.

When you live an ordered life your energy increases considerably. When you get up at around the same time daily and go to sleep at a similar time each evening your mind and body get into a rhythm. When you discipline yourself to exercise at the same time each day your body enjoys the regularity. When you do particular tasks or relax at around the same time each evening your body appreciates such organization.

But if you're always waking up at different times, changing your diet constantly, sometimes exercising fiercely and then doing none for weeks, your body won't function at its optimum level and your energy will be lower.

Don't get me wrong: I'm not advocating a boring robotic lifestyle. I'm just saying that a life without a good regular structure is not nature's way—and what goes against nature will not prosper in the long run.

If you're feeling down or lacking energy and direction, start by establishing some basic order in your life. Trust me—within a week you'll feel much better and your energy levels will rise substantially.

INCREASE MUSIC

One of the best things I do to raise my energy levels when I get into the office is to play uplifting classical music. Research shows that classical music (particularly baroque music) increases energy, makes you more creative, and actually increases your IQ score. Invigorating classical music in the morning is like an injection of vitamins for your brain. Music soothes the mind, enlivens the neurons, and helps make any human livelier and more energized.

The great thing about music therapy is that it's so easy. Just put on an album and it immediately begins to work its magic. Playing something uplifting for 20 minutes when you arrive at work will boost your energy levels and optimism.

You home should be full of inspiring, relaxing music too. It really is worth the time to visit music websites or ask your friends which artists they really get a kick out of listening to. Soon you'll develop an impressive library of music that you can play whenever you need to improve your energy.

Music has been part of human culture since people in caves started hand-clapping together. It affects us deeply at a psychological and even molecular level. Working on your personal menu of music will enhance the quality of your daily work and home life. A life without great music is unlikely to be an inspiring one.

REDUCE COFFEE

Coffee is great for improving thinking. Research shows clearly that mental performance improves after a cup of java. Not only that, many athletes report that they perform better when they ingest some caffeine half an hour before they need to perform.

However, I advise against having more than one coffee a day, for two reasons. The first is that after the coffee high you get the coffee low. A few hours after that latte your energy levels will be lower than before your first sip. In many ways coffee "borrows" energy from the future. Once you start using coffee as a mental performance enhancer it's hard not to get into the habit of having more cups during the day. Pretty soon your body finds it hard to perform well unless there's coffee inside it.

The second reason not to drink too much coffee is how it affects your hormones.

A while ago I was lucky enough to score a ticket to a medical professionals' conference featuring Dr. Thierry Hertoghe, one of the world's most renowned hormone experts. During question time at the seminar Dr. Hertoghe was asked what the worst danger to the human hormone system was. He answered with just one word: "Coffee." He then said that the human hormonal system is extremely delicate, and the smallest change in what we eat or drink affects it.

He asked us to imagine an Olympic-size swimming pool, then imagine that we had thrown a pinch of salt into that pool. He said that if the pool represented the body's hormonal system, and the salt was a hormonal change, then that tiny change would be immediately detected by the body's system. We are that sensitive to hormones.

Dr. Hertoghe believes that we have to be very careful not to alter our natural hormonal balance too much by what we eat and drink, and that coffee is one of the worst offenders.

So be careful. By all means have your daily cup of coffee, but don't let it become your daily three or four cups. Your energy levels will suffer if you do.

POSITIVE SELF-TALK

Here's a super-powerful way to keep your energy levels high: talk to yourself positively throughout the day. Whenever you're walking down the street, getting into an elevator or having a few moments alone, give yourself a mini motivational talk. One warning, though—don't move your lips, or people will think you've gone mad!

I do it all the time. I take a few moments to refocus on the type of person I want to be. I get clear on my goals. I tell myself this meeting will go fantastically, or that I am a top performer. You may feel a tad uncomfortable talking yourself up this way, but I assure you it really works. Your brain responds to almost any command you give it. Emphatically tell it it's happy and it will indeed get happier. Tell your brain you are full of energy and sure enough, your energy will increase. But say nothing to your brain all day long, and pretty soon it slips back into negative thinking patterns.

The trick with positive self-talk is to do it consistently. The first few weeks it will take some effort but then it will become a habit. Soon you'll become your own personal coach, pepping yourself up constantly. And your energy and enthusiasm will skyrocket as a result.

Remember: you are what you think about most of the time. Discipline yourself to think only constructive, empowering thoughts and your life will just get better and better. Let negative self-talk get hold of you and it doesn't matter how rich and successful you are, you will be miserable.

I believe how we think about ourselves and how we talk to ourselves are two of the most important success factors of our entire life. It's worth the effort to get them right.

DRINK GREEN PLANTS

One of the best energy enhancers is green vegetable juice. Whether it is spirulina or wheatgrass, barley, spinach, or celery, green plants consumed daily as juices can be huge energy boosters.

Don't worry—you don't have to buy bags full of veggies and crush them yourself. Just buy them in powdered form from your local health food store. How did I find out about the magical power of powdered greens? Well, one day I walked into my local health food store and asked the owner, "If I could buy only one thing in this store to improve my health, what would you suggest?" He didn't need long to think about it. He immediately pointed to the condensed green vegetable drinks and said he and his customers had been using them for years with terrific results.

Give them a try for yourself.

BOOST YOUR ENERGY TO SKY-HIGH LEVELS

And there you have it. A whole menu of proven techniques, products, and strategies to lift your energy mentally and physically.

Just imagine if you used every one of these strategies. Rather than get a small incremental boost in your energy, your levels would go sky-high. You'd be able to work longer, be less stressed, think better, and feel happier. These energy-enhancing techniques alone could literally change your life.

not asking the right questions

The next area we'll look at has the potential to revolutionize your life—not in months, years, or decades, but in days.

There is a single force that guides your future. A simple, yet profoundly powerful force that shapes your health, the quality of your life, your material success, and your overall happiness. You apply this potent force daily, but often in ways that pull your life down to a lower level. Yet by becoming more aware of it, you could just as easily use it to elevate your life to astonishing peaks.

What is this all-important force sculpting your life? It's the quality of the questions you ask yourself.

Think about it. We are constantly asking ourselves questions like:

How could I earn more?
How can I get out of this situation?
Does he care for me?
What's the solution?

Where is my future?
What should I have for lunch?
What should I do today?

Et cetera, ad infinitum. When you think about it, you'll realize that your questions are often the creator of your actions. They are your life compass and the rudder of your future.

People who habitually ask themselves negative questions like "Why can't I ever get it right?" doom themselves to an unhappy, unsuccessful life. In contrast, those who train themselves to ask uplifting, inspiring, possibility-filled questions usually experience a life that is filled with hope, adventure, and high achievement.

You must be very careful about the quality of the questions you ask yourself. If you want a premium-quality life, you need to ingrain in your mind a series of high-quality questions that you regularly ask yourself—questions that support you in your attempt to create the very best life possible for you and the people you most care for. These habitual questions will help you stay on the right track, be more optimistic, and take the best daily actions to help you reach the life of your dreams.

In this chapter, we'll look at a series of questions that I have found incredibly helpful in my life. Whenever I pause from the daily hustle and bustle of life and ponder these questions, invariably I feel more centered and inspired, then motivated to reattack my life with greater energy and vigor.

Here are the life questions that I find so valuable.

1. What Are My Values?

What do I care about most in life? What do I value above all else?

When you're certain about your values, you live life with much greater clarity and, therefore, velocity. Have you ever asked yourself which you value most between health and career? What about family versus friends—which do you feel is the more important? Where does spirituality come in your hierarchy of importance? What about community, or contribution to society?

Strangely enough, most people have never asked themselves these crucially important questions. This is a shame, because if they did bother to get clear about their values, they may well realize that they are not actually living the life they aspire to. The moment you get clarity on your values you'll start living a much more dynamic and genuinely successful life. You'll put what counts first. You'll get those things done that you know are really important to your happiness and fulfillment.

Try this quick exercise now. I think you'll really enjoy it—it's usually very revealing. Take a piece of paper and write down the following values in order of importance to you:

Spirituality
Health
Family
Fame
Wealth
Personal development
Friends
Adventure
Relaxation

Once you've done this, you need to ask yourself one simple question: now that I have a ladder of values, am I currently living my life according to my most important ones?

The sad fact is that most of us aren't.

But the good news is it usually isn't that difficult to rebuild your life around your values. A change in lifestyle here, a reminder note there, are often all you need to get back on track. The key is to be aware of your value gaps and spend just a few minutes daily thinking about how you can bridge them. After all, a life lived in accordance with your most cherished values is a rich life indeed.

2. What Would I Do If I Knew I Couldn't Fail?

This is a classic question, because it gets to the very core of your self-image and life dreams. It forces you to take a long, hard look at what you want out of life and what you believe deep down you deserve.

Are you thinking too small? Are you putting unnecessary limits on your life?

Take a few minutes now and remove the shackles from your mind. What have you often dreamed about but just assumed was impossible to achieve? What would you really love to do with your life? Make a list of your wildest, most exciting dreams. Come on, try it now—it'll only take a few minutes.

Now ask yourself, are they *really* impossible? How could I make them happen? And furthermore, even if I couldn't achieve them would I learn a lot and have mountains of fun at least trying?

Remember: achieving a goal is not the most valuable part of the process. The satisfaction you derive from succeeding with a goal is often fleeting; what's really worthwhile is how much you grow as you stretch yourself to reach for the goal. The journey itself is the reward. So even if you take a shot at some wild dream and fail, the experience could be one of the richest of your entire life.

Attempting a humongously big goal has another advantage, too: it's a blast! It's one of the most exciting, invigorating, and fun-filled things you can do. It really gets you up in the morning, because you're going for something great.

The truth is, most people sell themselves short throughout their lives. Deep in their heart they don't really think they're that special; they settle for a fraction of their dreams. Don't be like this. Trust me: when you aim high, all kinds of forces come to your aid to help you along your path. You become vastly more passionate and stimulated by life when you're pushing yourself to achieve something momentous.

Even if you ultimately fail you still end up a winner. You'll have had some grand adventures and you'll probably have achieved much, much more than you would have if you had simply aimed low. Great success belongs to the dreamers of this world—but dreamers who work daily to make their golden dreams a reality, step by step.

3. What Could Go Wrong?

Such a simple question, but with such profound implications. I use this question regularly when I have big decisions to make.

Put it this way: the bankruptcy courts are full of people who failed to ask themselves this one basic question. It's easy, when we have an amazing idea or project, to get carried away with all the great possibilities that emanate from it. But what about the costs if all doesn't go as planned? Few people take the time to look at the downside, and they can pay dearly for that carelessness.

Get into the habit of asking yourself this fundamental question whenever you're at the crossroads of a major decision. I use the following system developed by Edward de Bono, the famous thinking expert, whenever I need to decide my future direction.

First I create three columns that look like this:

Positive	Negative	Interesting

Under the first column, I list all the positives of making a particular decision. Then I force myself to evaluate all the negatives and write them in the second column. (Generally there is no decision that doesn't have at least some negatives if you think deeply enough about it.)

Often after filling out the Negatives column I decide the venture is not for me. But if I'm still unsure, I progress to the Interesting column.

This is a really clever idea of de Bono's. In the Interesting column you list all the less obvious aspects of the situation—other people's thoughts, situations that may be similar to yours, what your intuition says, and so on. Often it's the Interesting column that really makes your pathway clear. I find it usually helps clarify my position pretty quickly and adds much more depth and texture to my thinking.

It's crucial to work at analyzing problems rather than rushing off and going ahead with projects just because it all looks good at first glance. If everyone regularly asked themselves "What could go wrong?" there'd be a lot less failure in the world, that's for certain.

4. How Could I Make 10 Times More Money?

It takes a certain amount of courage to treat this question seriously. Many people scoff at the notion that it's even possible to earn 10 times more than they currently do. But that's exactly what makes the question so potent.

Asking yourself this question gets you out of your comfort zone; it really stretches your boundaries. It forces you to think far bigger than you may ever have before. You can't earn 10 times more by making a few small incremental improvements at work—you have to revolution-ize the way you produce results.

Suspend disbelief for a moment and imagine that you could actually achieve this. How would you do it? What would you have to learn? Who would you need to partner with? What type of person would you have to become?

The reality is that millions of people in the world have increased their income 10 times in just a few years—why not you? Plus, even if your answers don't reveal a road to being 10 times richer, I bet you get some cracking ideas on how to lift your earnings by at least two or three times.

That's the power of the 10× question—it leads to quantum rises in the quality and quantity of your output. Let's face it: we are much more likely to underrate our abilities than to overrate them. Most humans have too little confidence, not too much. Asking yourself this question helps you to let go of your insecurities and push yourself to new heights.

It can be applied outside the business arena, too. Ask yourself how you could improve your love life 10 times (there could be some interesting answers!). Or your fitness. Or your intelligence. Or your happiness. I think you'll be pleasantly surprised at some of the solutions you arrive at.

5. What Would X Do?

This question is terrific when you find yourself in a tricky, complex situation you're having difficulty solving.

It's a simple technique. All you do is think of someone you admire or who is renowned in your field and ask yourself what they would do if they were in the same situation. Literally pretend you are them for a few minutes. How would they strategize? What tactics do you guess they would employ? What would their attitude be on an issue like this one?

Sometimes if I have a serious business problem I ask myself, "What would Jack Welch do?" (Welch was the legendary CEO of General Electric and is universally regarded as one of the finest chief executives in corporate history.)

Putting yourself in someone else's shoes frees up your mind to think in new, fresher ways. If you really get into it, pretty soon a whole flood of solutions and points of view will come to you—ways of thinking that you would not normally conceive.

I liked to use this technique when I was writing advertisements professionally and got stuck on a brief. I would pick two or three of the world's greatest ad writers, then act like I was them. It felt a bit silly at first, but sure enough after a while I started thinking more like them and less like myself. It often led to some excellent solutions.

In his brilliant 1937 book *Think and Grow Rich,* Napoleon Hill advocated creating a mastermind group of people throughout history who could help you come up with solutions. Hill's technique was to get readers to close their eyes and imagine they were in a meeting with these luminaries of history. You put whatever problem you had to the group and imagined what their answers would be. I've tried this method a few times and found it to be an effective way of unlocking my mind and opening myself up to novel solutions.

Finally, I have used this technique on occasion when giving speeches to groups. I regularly speak to organizations interested in my ideas on high performance, entrepreneurism, marketing, and motivation. Sometimes before I go on stage, I'll think of one of the world's top public speakers and envision I am like them in ability. Invariably it lifts my speaking performance up a notch.

This technique is particularly apt when you find yourself in a field you don't know much about. Why not get advice from the experts, even if it's occurring purely in your mind? It all helps.

6. Should I Even Be Involved with This?

This question uses a technique known as zero-based thinking. Using ZBT you periodically question at the most basic level any activity or project you're involved with.

Simply ask yourself, "If I were starting over again, would I choose to be doing this?" It's a great question to ask because often we do projects, work in companies, or hang out with people purely because we are used to doing so. It's habit. The question challenges you to look more freely at your situation, urging you to cease being involved with it if it no longer serves you.

It can be a tough question to ask because it often leads to some uncomfortable answers. It may make you quit your job, move from your hometown, see less of certain friends, or even leave your partner. But regularly practicing ZBT ensures that your time is spent on activities that are valuable and pertinent to you. It stops you slipping into ruts, doing things just because they've always been done that way. If we're honest with ourselves most of us will admit that we are dragging a few things into our future that should have been left in our past.

I'm not suggesting that you coldly throw away people and companies that are important to you just because they've been around for ages, but merely that you prune the tree of your life, getting rid of situations and circumstances that bring no value to you at all. Or that were right for you once, but only slow you down or inhibit you now.

Why not take a look at where you work currently. If you could do it all over again, would you choose to work there? What is making you stay?

What about your personal life? If you could start again from scratch, would you involve yourself in the same lifestyle you currently have? If you wouldn't, how could you change things so that they enhance your life and make it more fun and satisfying?

Powerful questions. Questions well worth asking at least every six months or so.

7. How Could My Competition Defeat Me?

When things are going well it's easy to sit back and relax. But constant vigilance is needed if you are to maintain your place in society or in the business world. It's when life is nice and easy that you must pay the most attention to possible weaknesses and flaws that your competition could exploit to their advantage.

Try this quick exercise. Imagine that you work for your competitor. How would you beat your company? Where are your weak points? Where don't you stack up against the competition? Make a list of 3–5 areas where you're not absolutely superlative, then come up with ways to improve them.

Constant refinement and innovation are compulsory if you are to remain at the top of your industry. Discover your flaws before other people do, then eradicate them before your competition even knows they exist. That is the secret to long-term superiority.

So many people just rely on their personal talent to get them through life. But if you want to be an elite performer you must repair any chink in your armor, even if you appear to be ahead of the game. The world is always changing, and new competitors are always arising. If you're not constantly improving yourself then you are in very real danger of slipping behind.

8. What's the Best Use of My Time Right Now?

Frankly, just asking yourself this one question throughout the day has the capacity to dramatically improve your life by itself. It's the question all highly effective people are constantly asking themselves, consciously or not.

This basic question can be a rudder for your whole life. Keep coming back to it again and again and you'll see it work its magic on your results. It forces you to get back to doing what's important, not just what is urgent or what pops up in your e-mail.

Can time management be this simple? You bet it can. Get good at asking this question and you'll need little more to outperform your competition. It quickly stops you from being lazy and doing unimportant things.

When you think about it, in today's fast-moving world busyness is a given. We are all busy. But being busy doesn't mean that you're getting important things done—although most people behave as if it does. Society admires hurrying, but to be effective you should focus on the best use of your time, not just be busy for the sake of it.

The best use of your time may not be being in a hurry at all. It may be thinking. It may be relaxing. It may be making just one important call, or reading one highly relevant magazine article carefully. If all you did at the beginning of each day was choose one task that was really valuable, and get that done, a year later you probably would have enjoyed the most productive year of your life.

The great thing about this question is that it's not about quantity, it's about quality. And it points the way through the jungle of to-dos toward the one or two tasks that really count.

It's not just relevant to your career. You can ask yourself this question to maximize your social life or even your relationships. Maybe the best use of your time is to hug your son. Or plan a much-overdue family get-together. Or book a romantic weekend away.

Only you know the answer in your heart. But keep asking "What is the best use of my time right now?" and you will not long be able to avoid addressing the answers. You will achieve at a higher level and become more relaxed. In addition, as you get more vital things done, your self-esteem will soar, and your happiness will skyrocket.

9. When I Die, What Kind of Life Would I Like to Have Lived?

Most people hate thinking about death. But keeping death regularly in mind is one of the very best ways to ensure a wonderful life. The thought of death is the world's greatest wake-up call.

Perhaps you've seen TV shows about people who changed their whole life when they had a near-death experience. Just the thought that their life could end was enough for them to suddenly realize that it was time they made some big lifestyle changes.

You don't have to have a near-death experience to get its benefits. Just regularly ask yourself "When I die, what kind of life would I like to have lived?" and you'll make many of the changes you need to.

What do most people wish for on their deathbed? Well, as the saying goes, "When they are about to die, nobody wishes they'd spent more time at the office." Research shows most people wish they'd:

Taken more risks
Had more fun
Loved more
Spent more time with friends

Interesting, huh? Looking at that list now, how does your life stack up against it? If you're like most of us, you'll realize that maybe you're spending too much time on work stuff and not enough time on enjoyment. That's understandable. The demands of work life can be substantial, and the pressure to provide a decent lifestyle for yourself and your loved ones is very real. But don't let society's increased demands stop you designing your life so it's holistically great and not just good in one or two areas. Normally the areas we are deficient in are joy, love, health, spirituality and fun.

Sadly, many of us spend fifty years merely making a living rather than designing the life of our dreams. But for all of us will come that time just before death when we finally see our life with absolute clarity. Will we be worrying about how much cash we have made? The size of our home? How successful we have been compared to our peers?

Hardly. We'll be reminiscing about all the moments of joy shared with people we love. And you know that's the truth.

10. How Could I Improve That Performance?

The Blue Angels of the U.S. Navy are the most famous aerial acrobatic team in the world. For over sixty years they have thrilled Americans with their precision flying and death-defying air stunts.

Their excellence is a result of literally thousands of hours of practice. The pilots know their routines to the nth degree and could almost do them in their sleep. This is why it is so surprising to observe what the Blue Angels do after every single performance.

They go back into their barracks and review every move they made, in the greatest detail. It's a philosophy that has been drilled into the best military units in the world, and many training experts believe it's one of the primary reasons they perform at such a high level.

Without incessant performance reviews, excellence just won't happen—not just for the Blue Angels, but for any team or individual. Funny thing is, outside the military, very few people carry out a detailed review of how they or their team performed immediately after an event.

Yet high-achievement experts like Israel's Yehuda Shinar have shown that the technique is as relevant for civilians as any military unit: "This continuous evaluation of performance helps winners to identify how they can increase the frequency of success and decrease the frequency of failure. Debriefing comes naturally to winners because they have a fundamental, self-driven desire to be in a constant state of improvement."

That's why "How could I improve that performance?" is such a terrific question to regularly ask yourself. It focuses you on making the tiny, gradual improvements that eventually make the difference between a satisfactory result and a superlative one. Ask it daily, and over time it will help lift your performance to a truly superb level.

AN IMPORTANT EXERCISE

Those are the 10 most powerful questions to ask yourself if you want to get more joy and achievement out of your life.

Be sure you take the 15 minutes or so to answer them before you go on to the next chapter. Remember: this book only works if you do the exercises it contains and make them a part of your life.

In addition, scribble the 10 questions on a piece of paper and keep it where you'll look at them every month or so. They can be like a compass that points you in the right direction at various crucial points in your life.

I think you'll agree that a life built with these 10 questions in mind would be a rich life indeed.

poor presentation skills

There is one subject that should be compulsory in every school: presenting well.

I t's such a vital tool of living, yet many bright, talented, dedicated people never get as far in life as they'd like because they can't present to a high standard.

The fact is, people do judge by appearances. If you have great ideas but present them poorly, many people will fail to see their worth. You'll often be beaten by somebody whose ideas are less worthy than yours, but who presented them superlatively.

Great presenters always go further in life because their awesome presentation powers make them look far smarter than they may actually be. Because they express themselves eloquently, people marvel at them, assuming them to be among the wisest of the wise. Of course, sometimes people see through all the eloquence and showmanship, but just as often they do not. The packaging becomes the reality.

Now imagine what life would be like if you were both very smart *and* a great presenter. The world would be pretty much yours for the taking!

Many people are terrified of giving presentations. Indeed, research shows that large numbers of people rate speaking in public more scary than death. Ridiculous but true.

If you find presenting a struggle or if you'd just like to become a master of presenting, I have good news for you. In this chapter I'm going to give you a list of the best tips I have ever learned about giving knockout presentations. I'll also give you some little-known advice about preparing yourself mentally before an event so you don't start shaking with fear.

I have a confession. I used to be terrified of speaking. Some may find that hard to believe, as I now regularly get paid several thousand dollars just to give a 45-minute speech—but it's true. In fact, I hated public speaking so much that I had trouble concentrating on my work for several days before I spoke.

If I can learn to present well, you sure can. All you need are the right tools, a bit of faith, and plenty of practice. Let's get into some tips for presenting superbly.

THE CLASSIC PRESENTATION

The first tip is to use the Classic Presenting Structure. This is a very simple framework you can build all your presentations around. It makes it easy to plan a speech.

1. *Tell them what you're going to say.* Let them know what the speech is about with a brief summary or encapsulation upfront. For a meeting it's usually an agenda, or a slide on your computer outlining what you'll be talking about. For a wedding speech it might be something like "The groom has some very interesting character traits I'm sure you'd like to hear about. Well, first of all . . . " This elementary structure sets up the main body of your presentation quickly and clearly.

2. *Say it.* This is the heart of your presentation. It's where you lay down your main points for your audience's consideration. I'll give you lots of help for making this part memorable a little later in the chapter.

3. *Tell them what you just said.* In this section of your presentation you summarize what you've been talking about, bring it all together, and finish.

Now the three-step structure may look pretty obvious, but many presenters don't use it and end up giving muddled, repetitive, or just plain confusing presentations. Stick with this structure and it's hard to give a bad speech.

VERBAL PRACTICE MAKES PERFECT

The next trick to giving awesome presentations is to practice aloud. It really makes a gigantic difference. Practicing aloud enables you to see how long the speech takes to go through, forces you to express your thoughts far more clearly, and makes you less nervous when it comes to delivering the real thing. Furthermore, when you practice your presentation aloud you'll realize flaws in your arguments and will better see where the breaks and pauses should occur within the speech.

Practice in your mind only and you'll miss out on all these advantages.

COMMUNICATE EYE TO EYE

I've seen businesspeople lose accounts because they only addressed one or two people in a boardroom and consequently offended the others, to whom they gave no eye contact. Remember: even if someone is junior, it doesn't mean they are not influential in the decision-making process. Everyone should get your attention every minute or so when you're talking.

Speaking experts know that the best way of establishing eye contact is to pause for a second or two and look one person straight in the eye, and then move on to the next person. That makes people feel as if you are specifically addressing a point to them, rather than to everyone in the room. It makes them feel valued.

Improve your eye contact and you'll be vastly more persuasive. It's one of the main areas that separates average presenters from outstanding presenters.

PAUSE. WHEN. YOU. SPEAK.

Another area that masters of presenting are aware of is the power of the pause.

Pausing at the right time can triple the impact of what you say. When you pause, the audience often leans forward to hear what you are about to say, their interest increased. Pausing helps you emphasize important points, too.

Frequent pausing also makes your speech appear more interesting and varied. It makes you seem more compelling and easier to listen to. A pause at the end of each section of your presentation allows time for your points to sink in.

The intelligent use of pausing can vastly improve the overall memorability of your talk. As the old saying goes, "It's the space between the notes that makes the music."

Take a look at the world's greatest speakers in history. View videos of John F. Kennedy, Winston Churchill, Martin Luther King Jr., and the top motivational and inspirational speakers, such as Denis Waitley, Anthony Robbins, and Robin Sharma, and you'll see pausing is a fundamental part of each one's speaking style.

VARY YOUR VOICE

The same is true of voice modulation. There's nothing that will send an audience to sleep faster than a person who speaks in a monotonous voice. It makes everything they say sound the same and can be very tedious to listen to. Modulate your voice, sometimes speaking slowly, sometimes fast, sometimes seriously, sometimes more lightly.

Treat your speaking like a well-written song, or even like a movie. Keep the pace and style varied and your audience will be captivated by what you say. The changes shouldn't be extreme—they should be subtle, barely noticeable unless the listener is actually trying to spot them. Although they will be minor variations, together they will play a large part in improving your delivery impact.

GET OBJECTIVE FEEDBACK

One of the best ways to improve your presentation style is to get someone else to critique you.

After you've prepared your presentation, grab a friend you trust, and deliver your talk to him or her. Ask your friend to look for flaws and watch out for inconsistencies. You'll be amazed at how many little mistakes you make when presenting that you yourself would never pick up, yet others watching can immediately identify.

Of course, some of us don't enjoy having others point out mistakes in what we're doing. But let's face it: some of the most important moments of your life will be presentations of one sort or another, whether a speech to your loved ones or a talk to a giant corporation when you're trying to win big business. Isn't it better to be a little uncomfortable being critiqued by a friend or associate than to deliver a flawed presentation to a real audience?

As they say, practice makes perfect. But practicing in front of others is another level above.

SEE YOURSELF AS PERFORMING WELL

Sometimes you can practice your speech fully, know every word of it, and still fall apart when you're on stage.

Often that's because deep down in your mind, you don't think you can pull off the presentation. You keep imagining that you're going to fluff your lines, stammer and stutter, or in some way make a fool of yourself.

That's why it pays to not just practice your speech aloud but also practice it in your mind.

On the day of any speech I have coming up, I visualize myself giving a superlative presentation. I close my eyes and see a picture of myself speaking strongly and warmly. I see the audience reacting well, enraptured by what I'm saying. Sometimes I view the scene from my point of view on the stage and other times I see myself from the audience's point of view.

The more I visualize my speech going well, usually the better it goes. Visualization is even more potent if you can take a few minutes before the presentation starts and do your mental rehearsal in the actual room you'll be speaking in. When you mentally rehearse on stage you feel even more confident. Your feelings of nervousness will be halved once you're up there behind the lectern seeing yourself in your mind giving a brilliant speech.

When I am standing at the back of an auditorium, only minutes away from being called up on stage, rather than fretting about whether my speech will go well I like to do one last visualization. I find that now I can see the audience, this visualization is the most powerful of all. It has a realism to it that can't be duplicated when you're doing mental rehearsal back at your office or home.

All the great speakers constantly visualize their speech going well in their mind as they practice. They see themselves relaxed and dynamic on stage. They see the audience hanging on their every word, then giving them an ovation. And they imagine feeling delighted with their speech at its conclusion.

Make visualization a permanent part of your speech preparation system and watch your speaking performance soar.

PRACTICE USING YOUR HANDS

What a difference this makes. The use of hand gestures during a speech can improve your impact at least another 20 percent.

When you use your hands well, it makes your speech more lively and dynamic. It makes you look as if you're much more enthusiastic, too. When I see people speaking with their whole body, particularly their arms and hands, I find myself drawn into what they are talking about. It gives me the impression that they really care about and believe in what they are saying.

A speaker who uses his or her hands emphatically can really lift the energy of the whole room. Look at old film footage of Adolf Hitler during World War II. Even when you can't understand a word he's saying he rivets you with the power of his delivery, largely because of his dramatic hand movements as he speaks.

Of course, I don't suggest you mimic the speaking style of that tyrant—just that as you practice your presentation, also rehearse hand movements for various moments of it.

Try to develop a repertoire of five different hand movements, practicing them enough so they become a part of you without your having to think much about them. Then look at your speech's three most important parts. Which of those hand movements could be used at those moments to really slam home your point? Rehearse those hand gestures for those key moments.

When you first start using your hands deliberately throughout a presentation it may feel a little weird. But after you've done it a few times you'll find it becomes totally natural to you. Then, when you look back on how you once presented without such movements, you'll realize your delivery wasn't nearly as impactful.

Of course, many of the professional speakers who travel the nation giving two or three speeches a week don't just use their hands. They come out from behind the podium and walk right across the stage, throwing their whole body into their presentation. But most readers of this book will be stationary for their speech, which will often be in a conference room. So becoming expert in using hand movements is the only physical movement technique you need to learn, in my view.

By the way, a good way to find out which hand movement works best for you is to practice in front of a mirror.

MEMORIZE YOUR START AND FINISH

Generally speaking, I am not a believer in writing every word of a speech. Reading it out can make the speech seem a bit stilted and labored—and each time you look down at it you lose eye contact with your audience.

I'm much more a fan of making notes of your main points and speaking from those. It takes a bit of practice, but the end result is a speech that is smoother and often appears more genuine and natural.

However, I do believe it makes sense to first have every word of your beginning and end down on paper, and then memorized so that you can repeat them word for word.

Why? Simply because the start and finish are absolutely crucial moments of your speech and shouldn't be left to chance. When you've thought about every word of your speech's beginning and conclusion, you can be more sure they will come across in exactly the way you intend. What you say at the start and finish is usually what your audience will remember most. Do those bits brilliantly and an average job on the rest and most people will still think of your presentation as a good one. Have a poor start and a limp conclusion and the overall impact of your entire presentation will be greatly diminished.

When I say memorize the beginning and end, I don't mean that you have to remember the first and last 5–10 minutes—just the first and last minute will do. That's enough to ensure that you start and finish well.

Committing the beginning and end of your presentation to memory will also increase your confidence. Even if you've got butterflies in your stomach as you first stand up to talk, because your opening sentences are memorized it will be easy to deliver them without thinking much about them. Then as you near the end of your talk you'll have rising confidence knowing that you've got a great ending coming up.

INCLUDE STORIES

I remember asking a friend of mine who ran seminars for a living about the secret of a great speech. He gave me a one-word answer: "Stories."

The more I studied public speaking the more I appreciated his point. People love hearing stories. Good stories have played a significant part in world culture since humans learned to talk. When you make a point with an interesting analogy or story, people tend to understand it more easily. They're more likely to remember it, too. When they go home and their partner asks what your presentation was like, they're likely to repeat just one or two stories you told rather than a complete outline of your talk. Stories captivate the listener and enliven and uplift a speech from the rational level to the emotional level—and what we feel emotive about, we remember.

A good way to write a presentation is to list the 3–5 main points you are aiming to address. Then underneath each point write a story or interesting example to bring that point to life. That way, you're blending the rational with the emotional in a balanced way. Speeches that consist almost entirely of stories can appear a bit fluffy and shallow, and presentations that drily enumerate their points of argument usually come across as boring. But switching from rational points to stories, back and forth, makes your presentation both entertaining and useful.

If you have trouble thinking of relevant stories, look back into your history. How did you solve similar issues before? What did other people do when faced with the same challenge? You should be able to think of several examples or stories just by asking yourself these two questions. Remember: your stories don't have to be earth-shattering, just interesting, memorable, and relevant.

As you start focusing on placing stories at the heart of your presentations, you'll find good stories that can be used again and again. Soon you'll have a menu of great stories that fit the topics you're asked to speak about. Then creating an entertaining, poignant presentation will be almost effortless; you'll just build it around two or three key stories in your repertoire.

ARRIVE EARLY

I've seen many presentations ruined because the person arrived only at the time of their speech, not earlier. As a result they were flustered and anxious, with their presentation material often out of order. They started poorly and usually never recovered from the bad impression that such a beginning gave the audience.

Even worse, they arrived after everyone else was already in the meeting room, and the audience had to wait as they booted up their computer and slide show. It was uncomfortable for everyone, especially the speaker.

It's an easy mistake to avoid. Just aim to be fully ready 15 minutes before your presentation begins. If you're presenting at someone else's office, ask if you can arrive early to set up. If you can't, then boot up your computer at a nearby café and walk into the room with it warmed up and ready to rock. Then just plug it into their system and you're all set.

If you're speaking in an auditorium or at a seminar, arriving early has other benefits. Firstly, it will relieve the organizers immensely to know that you've arrived well before you're due on stage (it silently says that you are a top-notch professional, too—someone they can trust with future gigs). It also gives you time to scope out the room and get a feel for the ambience and tone of the event.

Whenever I speak at a seminar, I like to arrive just before the break for morning coffee or lunch, or if I'm the first one speaking, a good hour before I'm due to speak. This allows me to meet the sound team, check my microphone audio level, and even practice a few minutes of my speech up on stage. This dramatically increases my confidence and makes me feel much more at home.

Ideally I like to arrive early enough that I can chat with other delegates. It helps if you get to know your audience beforehand, and it's amazing how often you can find out a small morsel of information that can alter what you eventually say in your presentation.

I had to learn the arriving-early lesson the hard way. Several times a plane delay or heavy traffic made me late for a big meeting. It's a very stressful feeling for all concerned. These days I try to force myself to leave for the presentation early enough so that even if I have travel problems and it takes me longer than I imagined to get to the venue, I still arrive with plenty of time to spare. I can't tell you how often I've needed every minute of that extra time.

STUDY THE GREAT SPEAKERS

As in any field, you can only be a truly great speaker if you learn from the greats. This is easier said than done. It's actually not that easy to identify truly superb speakers; a lot of them don't have huge public profiles.

So here is a collection of speakers who not only are truly awesome but have audio or video copies of their speeches available, often on their websites.

Og Mandino. Although he is now deceased, it's worth getting hold of any of Og's one-hour keynote speeches. Originally famous for his first inspirational book, *The Greatest Salesman in the World*, Mandino subsequently became one of the most popular paid speakers in America. When you study his speeches, observe how well he uses pauses to hammer home his key points.

Brian Tracy. Brian has been speaking professionally for over twenty-five years and is a master of the craft. He uses what he calls the "Windscreen Wiper" model of speaking, switching throughout his speech from rational points to emotional/fun stories and anecdotes. He's a great example of how to speak in a conservative but still entertaining way.

Tom Peters. Tom reportedly gets paid around $100,000 to speak for a day. He's feisty, opinionated, always up to date, and quite riveting as a speaker. Tom is one of the world's best examples of how to use slides to great effect and how to deliver a business speech in a passionate way.

Bill Clinton. Try to get hold of former president Clinton's post-presidential speeches. He's looser, more forthright, more relaxed, but still electrifying. I saw him speak for an hour in front of a high-level audience of 1,000 in Sydney and the entire group sat transfixed by him. Watch footage of him and notice how effortlessly he weaves in relevant facts without ending up with an overly dry speech.

Robin Sharma. Canadian Robin Sharma is a couple of decades younger than the other speaking stars, and it shows in his more casual dress and Zen-like philosophical demeanor. Robin is excellent at telling stories in a compelling way and is great to watch if you are looking to deliver a high-level yet relaxed speech.

Remember: these people make their living giving speeches. They've spent years refining and finessing their delivery style and content. They've tested what works.

Jump on the Internet and track down some videos of their speeches. Analyze them, examine their structure. There are so many great lessons in a top-flight speaker's presentation. Get one good tip and it's surely worth the effort. (To watch a video of me discussing how to present more persuasively, visit www.whypeoplefail.org.)

ONE STEP AT A TIME

I hope this long list of speaking lessons isn't too stressful. You only need to pick one or two concepts to work with at first. Then, when you've mastered those, pick another to work on. Pretty soon you'll find the standard of your presentations has become exponentially better.

Once you get good at speaking and presenting you'll start loving it. You'll realize that you now have an important advantage over your competitors. The simple fact is that most people cannot present well, so when you walk into a room and dazzle the audience it will make a big impression on them, I assure you.

Presenting well will increase your confidence and your salary faster than almost any other skill. Your boss will want you to lead more and your clients will trust you more. Your entire business life will become more streamlined and your stress levels will diminish. You'll feel in command and in control, and others will sense that they're dealing with someone highly capable and dynamic.

But beware: as you develop into a hot presenter, you'll also hit a potential roadblock. Laziness. You'll get so good at presenting you'll often think you can wing it and walk in without your usual preparation. Don't risk it. Stick to the structure that works, and always prepare well in advance. Really do your homework before you ever step into the spotlight. In this day and age presentations are too important to be put at risk through poor preparation.

Make every presentation superb, and you'll be amazed at how far you go in life.

mistaking IQ
for EQ

Since it was first widely used on U.S. Army soldiers during World War I, the IQ test, or intelligence quotient test, has been highly valued by society.

The long-held belief is that the higher the IQ rating, the more intelligent the person is. The more intelligent the person is, the more successful he or she will be. Therefore, for decades a high IQ has been a much-treasured achievement. Many people boast about their high IQ, implying that it means they are somehow better than the rest of us. Conversely, many teenagers who are told they have a lower IQ than average assume that they will probably not achieve much in life, a belief that of course soon becomes a self-fulfilling prophecy.

In recent years, however, both the theory that IQ tests are valid ways of analyzing a person's intelligence and the notion that a high IQ means a high success level have taken a pounding.

Respected researchers like Howard Gardner, a psychologist based at Harvard University, have shown that the standard IQ test is a far too simplistic judge of what true intelligence is. Gardner pioneered the concept of "multiple intelligences" and says that we actually have eight different kinds of intelligence. Some are highly developed in us; others need to be trained to reach even an average level.

1. *Visual/spatial intelligence.* The ability of a boxing master like Muhammad Ali to avoid his opponent's strikes yet still punch him is an example of this. Those who have this intelligence as a strength have excellent awareness of the space around them.

2. *Musical intelligence.* Some prodigies, such as Wolfgang Amadeus Mozart, have an incredible aptitude for understanding and playing music, even as nine-year-olds. If you have this intelligence you may well be adept at writing and playing music, as well as appreciating it.

3. *Verbal/linguistic intelligence.* Some people considered to be stupid may in fact be highly intelligent but just not very good at expressing themselves. This kind of intelligence includes the use of language and the understanding of it. Typically, writers, orators, and lawyers are strong in this intelligence.

4. *Logical/mathematical intelligence.* I remember at my school there were students who would get almost perfect marks in our highest-level math class without ever studying. This intelligence is all about skill with numbers and the ability to analyze problems in a logical manner.

5. *Interpersonal intelligence.* We all have friends who are superb con-versationalists and who can somehow read people's moods and feelings with ease. Those with interpersonal intelligence work effec-tively with almost everyone they encounter.

6. *Intrapersonal intelligence.* These are the people who know them-selves very well—what they desire, what they're capable of, and how to talk to themselves in a productive, positive way. Such people have good working models of themselves in their minds and thus can regulate themselves well in daily life.

7. *Naturalistic intelligence.* People with this intelligence have a great sensitivity to nature and feel very at home in it. This intelligence

concerns a person's ability to recognize patterns in nature and relate well to their natural surroundings.

But it may not stop there. Gardner is currently investigating the possibility that even more types of intelligence exist. His point is that it's ridiculous to evaluate anybody's total intelligence purely from the traditional IQ test. The brain is far too sophisticated an instrument to be judged in such a shallow way.

The man who leads the attack on the theory that a high IQ ensures great success in life is Dr. Daniel Goleman, a renowned psychologist and workplace effectiveness expert.

Goleman evaluated over 500 corporations and twenty-five years of extensive research and concluded that IQ was not the main determinant of success in life at all. It was EQ. In fact, Goleman and his team have shown that your EQ is twice as likely to indicate your success in later life as your IQ.

So, what exactly is EQ?

Well, EQ is shorthand for emotional intelligence, or, in a nutshell, how effectively you exercise your emotions to serve you rather than hinder you. It is a very deeply researched area, but I'll summarize Dr. Goleman's main thoughts on the two areas of EQ: personal competence and social competence.

PERSONAL COMPETENCE

Personal competence is all about how you manage yourself. Someone with a strong EQ will show the following personal characteristics.

Self-Awareness

This is when you know your emotions and the effects of them. You can accurately assess your strengths and weaknesses.

For example, some people know they have a temper and others are unaware they have one. Some folks know they get intimidated by bullies; others aren't clear that they behave that way.

As a result of knowing your strengths, limits, and emotions, you tend to be confident about yourself as a whole. You have a strong sense of your own self, you like yourself, and you value your contributions to those around you. Furthermore, you're normally clearer than the average person about your goals, your fears, and what you most value in life.

People with strong self-awareness are very conscious of how their feelings affect their performance, both positively and negatively.

Self-Regulation

This is all about managing and controlling your emotional states and impulses to act.

When you have high self-regulation EQ you've got your emotions in check. You don't explode into anger easily, nor are you excessively moody. You have emotional self-control. As a result of this inner stability, you have considerable outer stability. You are trustworthy and deliver what you promise. You have a strong sense of integrity and rate honesty highly in your list of personal values.

You don't take the easy way out, or cut corners. You are conscientious and always keen to do your job carefully and well, better sometimes than even your peers would ever expect of you. Rather than blame others, you take full responsibility for your own personal performance.

Motivation

This category is pretty much as it sounds. Goleman discovered empirical proof that people who are goal oriented have higher success levels. No surprises there. But such people also show greater satisfaction with life.

These people exhibit a strong achievement drive. They set themselves challenging tasks that make them stretch to the edges of their abilities. Taking calculated risks gives them energy, although they are a long way from being gamblers. They'll typically do whatever they can to reduce uncertainty, but won't be intimidated by it either.

These men and women are ready and waiting to leap on any opportunities that come their way. Despite their clear ambition, they're usually not just out for themselves. They're quite happy to align themselves with the goals of the organization they work with, as long as they get rewarded along the way.

When the going gets tough, they're definitely not fickle friends. They are motivated to stay the course even when life is hard and obstacles abound. These people focus on their goals and rarely think about throwing in the towel.

SOCIAL COMPETENCE

There are two characteristics of the strong EQ person in this area of social competence: empathy and social skills.

Empathy

Being aware of others' feelings and fears and being able to understand them are fundamental aspects of the socially competent.

These people don't just understand other people's feelings—they genuinely care about them. Their empathy is not an act; they're interested in others' lives and situations and like to help them whenever they're able to do so. Any chance they can, those people with empathy love to lift up those around them, helping them improve their abilities and maximize themselves.

Typically, they're great at serving others, whether professionally or personally. They get a kick out of meeting a customer's needs, for instance. It comes naturally to them as they're often able to predict in advance what the people around them are looking for.

Those who show empathy love people—all kinds of people. They're usually able to get on with folks from all walks of life. Rich or poor, black or white, quiet or sociable—everyone is interesting to this type.

They are anything but naive, however. Indeed, they show considerable political savvy. They can pick the power players and deftly ride any power shift. It's all part of the empathetic person's ability to read emotional states brilliantly.

Social Skills

Aligned closely with empathy is the second social competence: social skills.

Those with this attribute are excellent at persuading others. They're the kind of people who can convince you of one point of view, then argue the opposite point of view equally effectively.

They're excellent listeners and are open to what others are saying. A great example of this is Bill Clinton. I have read many times of people who have met him saying things like: "When Bill talked to me I had his total attention. I felt like I was the only person in the room."

This skill really comes to the fore when there's an argument going on. Those with social skills are outstanding at resolving people's differences and completing business negotiations. As a result, it's no surprise that people look on them as true leaders—a position they are usually quite comfortable with. That's because they find it relatively easy to collaborate with others and get everyone to band together for a common goal.

People with great social skills aren't tyrannical leaders, either—quite the opposite. Because they enjoy nurturing relationships, they're prepared to invest the time it takes to gain people's trust and support, often at a deep emotional level. Once they've bonded strongly with others in a group, they go on to inspire and guide those others towards the collective goal.

HOW DO YOU SCORE?

So there you have it. Those are the five main areas of emotional intelligence. When you read through them, I think you'll agree it's hard to dispute that they are all character traits worth having, and no doubt you have many if not all of them already to some degree. Knowing how important they are to your future success, however, I think it's really worthwhile to take a moment now to give yourself a grade of 1 to 10 in the five areas. Once you get crystal clear about which areas you're lacking in, you can quickly develop a program to lift your EQ levels even higher. So in your mind or with a pen, mark yourself on the five aspects of EQ now.

Emotional Intelligence Evaluation

Self-awareness	____/10
Self-regulation	____/10
Motivation	____/10
Empathy	____/10
Social skills	____/10

How'd you do? Any score of 7 or above is pretty good in my view, but any level below that could be cause for concern. You can be sure that a low mark in any of the areas is like pulling the handbrake on your life. Undoubtedly a weakness in any aspect of EQ will show up at work or at home, in your interactions with others and in the speed at which you are achieving the results you desire.

If you're at all unclear on how to grade yourself, you could always scan this chapter of the book and e-mail it to two or three close friends or work partners. Ask them if they'll take a few minutes to rate you on EQ. You may well be surprised by how you score.

The test is simple, but its ramifications are very significant indeed. Think about it. If your emotional intelligence level has been proven to be vitally important to your future success in life (far more important than your IQ), lifting your EQ levels even 10 percent will have a major impact on the quality of your life and the level of success you achieve.

IMPROVING YOUR EQ IS WORTH THE TIME

For many people, working on their EQ could be far more advantageous than doing extra courses in their industry, crawling to the boss, working longer hours, or even getting a pay raise. Fine-tuning your emotional intelligence could literally improve almost every major area of your life, not to mention have a major positive impact on those around you.

It could, for example, make you an expert at understanding and mastering human emotions—a priceless skill. According to researchers Salovey and Mayer, those who have a strong EQ have an excellent handle on four different emotional abilities:

Perceiving emotions: the ability to perceive other people's faces and voices and recognize how they are feeling, as well as your own.

Using emotions: the ability to think well and problem solve effectively, and make best use of your moods.

Understanding emotions: the ability to be sensitive to and comprehend others' subtle and complex emotions.

Managing emotions: the ability to manage and regulate your emotions so that they save you, not hinder you.

So if that's important, how do you go about lifting your EQ levels?

Well, the good news is that Dr. Goleman has found that any EQ area can be improved, no matter how badly you may think you are performing in that domain at the moment. And in the next few pages, I'll give you some quick and easy methods that will help you reach the EQ levels you desire and deserve.

Be Consistently Aware

The first method is to write the area of EQ in which you have scored lowest on a small piece of paper or Post-It note and stick it where you'll see it often throughout the day. Good places include on your bathroom mirror, next to your computer, or even on your car dashboard.

Each time you see the words they will trigger a reminder in your brain to focus on that area of improvement. It seems such an elementary, basic technique, but I assure you it works surprisingly well. Awareness of a problem is a vital first step in changing it. If you rarely think about improving something, your mind will not work on it and progress will be slow. But think about it all the time and get reminded of it every hour or so, and inevitably your mind will start focusing on the issue and begin working on ways to get better at it.

In fact, the reason so few people achieve their New Year's resolutions is that they promptly forget about the promises they've made. If all they did was stick reminder notes around them, it would double their chances of taking action and eventually achieving their goals.

This is a crucially important point, not just for improving your EQ but for changing any area of your life. What you focus on will change. As success coach Robin Sharma says, "With better awareness you make better choices and with better choices you get better results."

Take a minute right now to write down your worst area of EQ on paper and put it where you'll see it constantly. Then prepare to be impressed by how quickly you improve in that area.

Feedback to Go Forward

Getting feedback is the next powerful way to improve your EQ. Goleman's research has shown that when people get feedback from others about how they're behaving, it carries over to empathy in many other situations in their life. In other words, when you're coached well, you can improve.

As Goleman puts it, "The good news about emotional intelligence then is that—unlike IQ itself—it can improve throughout life. In a serendipitous fashion, life offers chance after chance to hone our emotional competence. In the normal course of a lifetime, emotional intelligence tends to increase as we learn to be more aware of our moods, to handle distressing emotions better, to listen and empathize—in short, as we become more mature."

This is fantastic news, because many people believe IQ remains fixed for life (although brain expert Tony Buzan says that he actually lifted his IQ test results to genius level, largely through consciously developing his mind and getting good at doing IQ tests). With EQ it's different. You're in charge of how high your EQ is. You are responsible for whether you reap the rewards of a top-level EQ or not.

Regular feedback is one of the best ways to improve fast. Just approach some of the people you asked earlier to evaluate your EQ and get them to coach you when they see you doing well or poorly with any of the five aspects of EQ. Most will be happy to help you out; after all, they get the benefits of your rising EQ, too, in the improved quality of their daily dealings with you.

Keep Studying the Experts

The third way to improve your EQ is to devour the many books written about this fascinating branch of psychology. Goleman himself has written several, including his original breakthrough text, entitled simply *Emotional Intelligence*, and his excellent follow-up book for corporate life, *Working with Emotional Intelligence.*

In addition to Goleman's writings, there are numerous books on EQ. (I recommend *Emotional Intelligence 2.0* by Travis Bradberry, and *The Other Kind of Smart* by Harvey Deutschendorf.) You'll be inspired and intrigued by some of the excellent texts on the subject and its related field, social intelligence.

I'm sure that the more you read about EQ and social intelligence the more you'll become interested in and excited by the concepts. You'll learn heaps of techniques and strategies for maximizing your emotional intelligence, and the exciting part is that you'll be able to apply what you learn immediately and get almost instant results.

I can think of few areas of human development more worth studying than EQ. Master this one aspect of your psychological makeup and every part of your life will get better—your social life, your career, your level of happiness, and your personal satisfaction. And most definitely your romantic life.

It will also become clear to you why so many people with a high IQ fail in life. They've got the raw brain power but don't run their own mind in an optimum way, either with their internal thinking or their social interaction.

Best of all, this is not an overly complex concept that only scientific geniuses can fathom. The lessons of EQ are simple. It's a cinch to put them into practice in your own life the very day you learn them.

FOCUS FOR A MONTH

It's such a shame all schools don't teach the principles of emotional intelligence. Imagine the impact it could have on our society if students were marked and evaluated as much on their EQ scores as their exam results. Not only would schools be producing graduates with better emotional skills, but with their new EQ levels I bet many of them would get higher academic scores, too.

Imagine, too, if EQ were taught in the prison system. When eventually released, felons would be better adjusted and more prepared to enter society again, with much less chance of returning to jail.

Imagine if couples in troubled relationships not only knew the concepts of EQ but made them a central part of their lives together. Many rocky marriages could be saved.

Until all that happens, rest assured that the concepts of emotional intelligence can help you right now to improve your level of material success and to increase your happiness.

Resolve today to pick one area where you scored low in the EQ test, then work on that area solidly for a month. Then switch to another area of EQ you'd like to be superb at.

Little by little, bit by bit, you'll end up becoming a master of how to run your own mind and interact better with others of all ages, backgrounds, and dispositions. You'll become a black belt of the mind, with unshakable belief in yourself and confidence in your future. You can even teach EQ to your family, friends, and loved ones and thus improve your immediate environment to a substantial degree.

And never again will you be intimidated by those who boast about their high IQ results. You'll know that you understand a style of intelligence far more crucial to living a better quality of life. When it comes to everyday practical living, EQ beats IQ every time.

poor self-image

Have you ever wondered why some really intelligent, nice, hard-working people never get anywhere in life?

Or how some people who don't seem to work that hard and haven't got that much going for them seem to always have great luck and achieve the things they dream of?

I sure have. In fact, it's a subject that has intrigued and perplexed me for my whole adult life. Having spent decades investigating what makes people fail or succeed, I have to conclude that it essentially comes down to two basic areas.

1. *Behavior systems.* The actions some people do regularly over time end up giving them a totally different result from the average performer.
2. The *mental state* of a high achiever is fundamentally different from that of the ordinary person. They believe in themselves, have greater courage, and are generally more positive in their thinking patterns.

Arguably the mental component is the more important, as the condition of your mind is what gets you to consistently take action in the first place. Your mind drives your actions. When your mind is clear, committed, and empowered, you become virtually unstoppable. You achieve your goals more quickly and easily, you don't get disheartened by temporary setbacks, and your mood tends to be upbeat and optimistic.

So if having awesome self-esteem, courage, and positive thinking are so vital, how can you develop them? Well, I think there are several ways to build your mind into a potent force, and I discuss them in other chapters of this book. But there's one part of your mental makeup that I think is more important than all the others: self-image.

SELF-IMAGE RULES

If you don't have a healthy, strong self-image you can try as hard as you like but you'll probably never get the success you hope for—and you certainly won't enjoy life along the way.

Why is your self-image so important? Because it determines what actions you'll take and how you'll feel each and every day. Those daily actions over time determine your results in life.

Your self-image is like your mental operating software: everything you do stems from it. It's like your mental blueprint of what's possible for you.

If you dream mighty dreams, it's because your self-image says it's OK to do so. If you approach a person you like and ask him or her out on a date, it's because your self-image says you have a chance. If after countless failures you persist in trying once again for a goal, it's because deep down your self-image tells you that you're capable of making that goal a reality.

YOU GET WHAT YOU EXPECT

Be certain: your self-image is ruling many aspects of your life, telling you what you can and can't achieve, should and shouldn't do. It's like the thermostat in an air conditioner. Your self-image is set at a certain level and you perform according to that level.

For example, many salespeople who start the month slowly will dig up more sales near the end of the month just to get them back to the wage their self-image is used to. But it works the other way, too. If they find they're suddenly earning a fortune at the start of the month, they often unconsciously do things to ensure by the end of the month they are back down to around the same amount they usually earn. It sounds crazy, but just ask people in the sales business and they'll verify that it's true. This kind of self-image direction is happening all the time.

In the long run, you usually get what you believe you deserve. Not what you wish for, not even what you desire, but what you expect deep down. And your level of expectation is determined largely by your self-image.

The power of self-image is clearly evident with lottery winners. It's widely known that many people who win the lottery end up back down at their previous wealth level within a few years. Why? Well, partially it's because that's the financial level they see themselves at. Their self-image makes them uncomfortable with having millions of dollars; they don't feel it's right or deserved. So sure enough, after a while they do things that cause them to end up where they started (in fact, plenty of times they end up with even less money than they originally had).

Dr. Maxwell Maltz, a plastic surgeon who spent a good portion of his time remodeling the faces of people who thought they were ugly, found that his patients were similarly affected by negative self-image. In his wonderful book, *Psycho-Cybernetics*, which caused a sensation when it first came out in the 1960s, he shared a curious discovery: Even when he'd fixed patients' nose or ears so they looked fantastic, patients often still viewed themselves as being unattractive. Because their self-image was that they were not good-looking, no amount of plastic surgery could make them feel like they were. When they looked in the mirror they saw what their self-image directed them to see, regardless of the reality.

Dr. Maltz realized that what was needed was "plastic surgery for the mind." He began to develop a series of processes to enable anyone to re-sculpt their self-image into one that liberated them from negative feelings about themselves and empowered their future. He was delighted to discover that changing his patients' self-perception often made them feel more happy and content with their lives, regardless of what their outward appearance was.

I'll detail a couple of his best techniques a little later in this chapter.

ONE-MINUTE TEST

Right now I'd like to turn the spotlight on you. What is your self-image like? Take a minute now to mark yourself A, B, or C in the box below.

One-Minute Test

Self-image category	Self-ranking (A, B, C)
Career	
Love	
Socially	
Character	
Self-discipline	
Physical attractiveness	
Spiritual awareness	
My future overall	

Do you have a strong view of yourself, or are you harboring negative and destructive self-images that regularly sabotage your success in life?

It's a very interesting test, isn't it? If you're like me, you'll have discovered that you have quite a few different self-images for different parts of your life.

Some people have incredible confidence and pride in their abilities at work, but rank themselves low socially. Others have a high self-image when it comes to their physical attractiveness but may see themselves as very mediocre spiritually. Some don't really like their own character or don't see their future as being bright.

Don't worry if you've given yourself a C in several areas—many of us do. No one's perfect, certainly not me. Furthermore, it is very common for people to underrate themselves in many aspects of their lives. The fact that you have marked yourself down in one or two areas doesn't actually mean that you *are* that way. It simply indicates that you *perceive* yourself that way. Your perception may be wrong or grossly exaggerated (you'd be amazed, for instance, how many professional fashion models actually think they are ugly).

Now that you have identified some weaknesses in your self-image, however, you have the opportunity to spend a few minutes each day reconfiguring it so that it supports you in all areas of your life.

It's important that you understand that these beliefs (or mental imperfections) can be changed. They are usually just based on emotional events, experiences or habits of thought that you've had in the past. They need not be permanent features of your personality.

Perhaps you were embarrassed in math class at school when you were nine years old, and since then you have believed you are a dunce at math. Maybe you were laughed at in your twenties by a girl you approached at a nightclub and then you accepted that you were unattractive to women. Or possibly your father told you repeatedly that you'd never get anywhere in life and slowly your subconscious mind began to believe that opinion was a reality.

RUNNING OLD PATTERNS

Remember this absolutely crucial point: *you are not your thinking.*

Your thinking is often just habitual, an almost mechanical reaction to your life circumstances. Usually you think like you have thought in the past. Mind/body guru Dr. Deepak Chopra reports an amazing statistic about the power of habitual thinking. He says that research has proven that the average person has around 60,000–70,000 thoughts a day, which is pretty amazing, but the even more extraordinary fact is that around 70 percent of those thoughts are the same ones you had yesterday!

You believe that you're thinking new thoughts, but really you're largely just running the same thoughts over and over again in your head. What passes for original, fresh thinking is often just mechanical, highly conditioned thinking. This is only a problem if those regular thoughts are pulling you down, making you feel disempowered, or keeping you from taking action. Sadly, this is very often the case.

For now, just pause for a minute and appreciate the momentous impact of this concept: you may not be the person you think you are.

In fact, it is almost certain that you are not that person you perceive in your mind. You are highly likely to be greater, infinitely more talented, vastly more special than you are currently imagining yourself to be. The truth is, because of their low self-image most people are selling themselves too short.

Here's an interesting fact. Apparently if you put fleas into a closed jar, they will attempt to escape by jumping out. But of course the lid of the jar stops them. Again and again they'll try hitting themselves on the ceiling of the jar. Come back a day later and remove the lid, and you'll see a remarkable thing. The fleas will have adjusted their jumping so that they only leap to the height of the jar lid. Even though there is now no lid, they believe that their jumping height is limited and they cannot jump further, and so they cannot escape the jar. Their beliefs have limited their actions.

Please remember this when you evaluate your own abilities. Just because something was true once doesn't mean it is true now. Just because in the past you've been shy, lazy, foolish, bad-tempered, selfish, or a failure in some areas, it in no way means you can't be confident, effective, brilliant, patient, caring, and a massive success in the future.

Let's get down to the nitty-gritty of how to create a powerful, positive, life-enhancing self-image.

BOOST YOUR SELF-IMAGE THROUGHOUT THE DAY

Step one is to focus on boosting your self-image throughout the day. In life, what you think about will consistently expand in importance for you. You may accept that your self-image is important right now as you read this book, but if you don't focus on it regularly through the days ahead it's unlikely to improve.

A good way to do this is to set several times a day to think about your self-image and focus on lifting it up. For instance, you could set the goal of thinking about your self-image just before every meal. That way you'll be working on your mental self-vision at least three times a day.

You might set your watch to alert you each hour to uplift your self-image. Or maybe when you're in the shower each morning that could be your self-image focus time. Some people take the time to cultivate their self-image while on their daily run or down at the gym. (That's what I do. That way I make myself stronger physically and mentally simultaneously.)

It doesn't matter where or when; what matters is that you train yourself to do it daily, preferably at multiple times during the day. The more you think about building your self-image, the stronger it will get.

ACT THE PART

The second method is the "Act as if." This is a terrifically powerful technique, proven to work by many thousands of people going as far back as Aristotle, the ancient Greek philosopher.

It's really simple. When you're thinking about your self-image, act as if you are already the person you wish to be. Create the ideal you in your mind, see it vividly, then behave like you are that person. Literally pretend that you are a top actor and that you are training for a big role. Practice all day being the person you want to be and you'll soon begin to become more like that person.

At first you may feel a little silly doing this, but if you persist with it I guarantee that within three days you will start feeling like you are actually becoming your ideal self. Three weeks later your behavior will be significantly altered. You'll be more confident, more relaxed, and performing at a higher level. Your new thinking will lead to new, better actions, which will lead to better results. By acting like your ideal version of yourself, your overall happiness will improve as your self-esteem rises to match your new self-image. Give it a go for a month and you'll be delighted at the results.

As I go about my day I often return to my vision of the person I would like to be, and then I try to behave like that person. Frankly, it can be tough sometimes. Plenty of times my ideal person is the opposite of how I'm feeling at that moment, so it takes considerable focus and willpower to get my mind back to that vision. But when I do, within minutes I'm feeling happier and performing better. It's remarkable how strong the connection is between what we think about and how we feel.

Over the last year I've trained myself so that whenever I get into my car my mind immediately starts thinking about the person I'd like to be. Try it yourself. It becomes habitual after a while and pretty soon you don't even have to remind yourself to do it—it just happens.

Now compare this way of thinking to that of the typical man or woman. Average people are pretty much puppets of their circumstances—when good things happen to them they feel good about themselves, and when bad things happen they feel bad. Their self-image changes with however they're feeling. Then when things get really tough they often emotionally beat themselves up, chastising themselves with negative thoughts about their self-worth and the type of person they are. This of course ruins their self-image. In reality, they let daily life create their self-image instead of firmly developing their own ideal self-image in their mind and sticking with it, no matter what life throws at them.

I'm not saying controlling your self-image is easy, but it is very possible. When you do, I promise you'll be rewarded with a giant leap in life satisfaction. Because the person with a strong, positive image will almost always feel better and perform better than the person with an unclear or negative self-ideal.

EMULATE YOUR FRIENDS

The next method of cultivating an outstanding self-image is to hang around with people who treat you like your ideal self-image, or who at least believe in and support you in becoming that person. The truth is, who you spend time with has an enormous influence on the person you become. Fraternize with lazy, weak-minded people and you'll slowly become more like them. Spend lots of time with upbeat, kind, high achievers and inevitably their attitudes will reflect onto you. You'll become more and more like them.

Unfortunately there will be lots of people reading this book who are trying to pull themselves up in life but keep getting pulled down by the people around them. This can be a particularly difficult situation when those people are part of your family. But you have to be strong and make sure you spend less time with these dark clouds and instead hang out with people who believe in you, admire you, and can help you get to where you want to be in life. It will make a huge difference to the quality of your life if you do.

Now I understand that in many cases it's not practical for you to totally abandon these negative influences on your life. (One may be your business partner, another could be your sister.) But that doesn't mean you have to spend day and night with them. Break away regularly. Give yourself large blocks of time away from them. Force yourself to find new, better-quality, more inspiring friends and associates. It's your life— be sure that you're living it with people of high caliber. If you don't, you'll find these emotional vampires will eventually affect you far more deeply than you may at first realize.

Your close associates are also often your advice panel, so it's vital they are smart, caring, and wise. Otherwise, the counsel they give may hurt you, not help you. Many successful people attribute their success to the quality of the people around them. Their close associates form a mastermind group they can rely on to help them when things turn sour and cheer them on when things are going well (as these successful people will then in turn do for them).

Take a minute now to consider the people you socialize with. Ask yourself:

Do they support me or pull me down?
Do I feel good around them?
Am I a better person in their company?
Can I rely on them when life gets hard?
Are they quality people?

If the answers are not resoundingly positive, then I recommend that you ditch them or, at the very least, see a lot less of them. Yeah, I know it's tough, but this is important. The only exception to the rule is "charity cases." You may elect to spend time with people who don't uplift you because you're there to help them, not worry about yourself. I applaud that attitude but still encourage you to make sure you balance that charity with time spent with people who make you feel good and bring out the best in you.

Look at anyone successful and you'll find they didn't do it alone. They usually had a support team of cheerleaders and wise counselors who helped them climb the slippery slopes of victory.

Be careful not to fall into the trap of rugged individualism. By that I mean telling yourself you can do it all by yourself, despite the human anchors around you pulling you downward. Although it may be possible, it's exhausting to have to do it alone. Get the right team behind you and every aspect of life becomes easier and success becomes much more likely—not to mention more fun.

PICTURE YOUR FUTURE

Now we come to the fourth way to enhance your self-image: the mentor board.

This can be a notice board, a wall of your home, your bathroom mirror, or even a scrapbook. Once you've found a suitable place, I ask you to fill it with pictures of people whom you would most want to be like. It could be pictures of top business executives, elite sports performers, great philanthropists, saints or spiritual masters, or even a mixture of all these types of people. Basically, put up anyone you admire and would like to emulate.

We all need inspirations—people we can look up to and try to be more like. If you know such people personally, all the better, but if, like me, most of your mentors are great figures of the world whom you've never met, then that's totally fine too. The main idea is make them a part of your life by putting pictures of them somewhere you'll see daily. This collection of champions will give you encouragement each day, every time you cast your eye on them. They're there to remind you to live your life at a higher level, with greater excellence and more substantial joy.

If you don't have such lofty role models in your life it's all too easy to compare yourself to the average people around you. But that's a low-standard way to live. You deserve great things in your life and you'll achieve them if you keep looking up, not around. That means picking awe-inspiring mentors, people who make you lift your game just by their example.

If you like, you can put more than people on your inspiration wall. You can post places you'd like to visit, the style of home or car you aspire to own, the type of body you're working to develop—anything and everything that helps you visualize the person you want to become, your ideal self-image.

In my own case, I like to stick these pictures on my bathroom mirror. That way each morning when I shave and each evening when I brush my teeth I'm reminded of the type of person I could and should be (and will be!). (I can tell you that friends who visit think I'm pretty weird when they see the mirror, but hey, it works for me.)

I must say, sometimes when the alarm clock goes off on a cold, dark winter's morning and I reluctantly stumble into the bathroom to begin my day, performing at a high level is the last thing on my mind. But truly, every time I look at that mirror and see that group of inspirational people looking back at me, it uplifts and energizes me. It's a great start to the day. It makes me think bigger and perform better, and gives me something to aim for. It's a wake-up call to make the effort to live the best life I can.

Try it for a month and see how you feel.

APPEARANCE AFFECTS FEELINGS

The next self-image enhancer is how you dress. It may seem a shallow thing to say, but the reality is that when you dress well you feel good about yourself. You feel more competent, more professional, more stylish, more like a winner.

Now I'm not suggesting you have to buy outrageously expensive gear—just high-quality clothes that you can afford but that make you look and feel special.

The way you dress affects you in subtle ways. I'm sure you have had plenty of times when you have worn something great and felt it improved both your mood and your self-image. If not, then it's definitely time to update your wardrobe! If you're short on cash, buy just a few items each year, but better-quality ones.

At the office, a good rule is to dress like the senior people in your company. The fact is, they are more likely to see you as one of them (and therefore promote you faster) if you look similar to them. So often I've walked past people in the city wearing such tacky clothes that I just know it's going to slow down their career progression.

Now remember: I'm not saying buy clothes you can't afford, just the best you can afford. It will be great for your career, but equally important, it will make you feel fantastic. And when you feel terrific you perform better. Simple as that.

THE POWER OF THE SELF-IMAGE TOOLKIT

In your self-image toolkit you now have a variety of techniques to lift up your confidence and keep you feeling good. You now know to focus on your ideal self throughout the day, to act like the person you want to be so that you eventually become more like that person. You know to get strict about the people you spend lots of time with, making sure they strengthen your self-image and don't break it apart. You've learned to create a mentor board to remind you to perform at a world-class level, and to dress like your ideal image so that you look and feel like a winner.

These are all simple techniques, but they're also seriously powerful ones. Practice just one of them every day and you'll notice an improvement in your self-image within a week. Do all of them and your self-image will be really something. You'll feel confident and in charge. Your performance will be dynamic and your results will be far beyond the ordinary.

Success will become easier, and come more naturally to you. You'll expect it, and feel deep inside that you deserve it. As you refine and develop a superb self-image, you'll also begin to appreciate that you are a very rare person indeed, someone who is taking control of your mind rather than letting the daily ups and downs of life determine your self-image.

In many ways, life is a mind game. Get your mentality in tip-top shape and superlative results are virtually inevitable. A strong, healthy self-image is the launch pad not just to a more successful life, but also to a happier one. It's not about being arrogant, but confident. Empowered. Inspired. And ready to deal with anything life throws at you, knowing deep inside yourself that you will not only survive, but absolutely thrive.

Believe in yourself and others will believe in you. Believe that you can do it, and that very belief will open up a world of magnificent possibilities.

not enough thinking

There's a disease sweeping cities throughout the world.

I call it Obsessive Do-itis. An absolute obsession with doing, doing, doing, rather than thinking, thinking, thinking. Running around frantically trying to squeeze in more meetings, more e-mails, and more activities into our ever-longer days.

It's reached ridiculous proportions. I was having coffee with a friend of mine who until recently ran the creative department of one of New York's biggest advertising agencies. He said that many days his diary would be completely full with meetings from 8 AM until 8 PM. And what did he do at 8 PM after all the meetings were over? He began his own work for the day.

It's crazy. It's also not productive. We are all kidding ourselves if we think that rushing around like mad people is getting more stuff done. It isn't. We're usually too frantic to think clearly, make the right decisions, and actually move things substantially forward. We have become intoxicated by working for work's sake. We are so inundated, so overwhelmed that many of us frantically start doing tasks as soon as we get into the office, in the hope that we can quickly lower our skyscraping in-tray.

Some hope. No sooner do we get a few tasks done than we're hit with an increasing bombardment of new to-dos.

A HIGH PRICE TO PAY

Worse still, in reaction to all this busyness some companies have developed a culture where they praise and admire incessantly busy people. To many, being busy equals being important. Being always unavailable means that you must be in demand, someone special. This kind of attitude merely makes those who are already busy work twice as hard. After all, it makes them look good and may well save their job.

The problem is not about to disappear any time soon. Quite the opposite. The avalanche of work is only gaining in speed and power.

As I see it, there are two solutions to the ever-increasing pressures of overload in today's society. The first is to become an expert at handling stuff (I've given you some good techniques for that in Chapter Three). The second is to avoid a lot of workload problems by nipping them in the bud early. The reality is that much of the mountain of work we have in front of us wouldn't even exist if we had done the right kind of thinking earlier in the week, month, year, or decade.

As a society we are suffering from a chronic shortage of thinking time. We are simply not allocating enough time in each day to sitting back and doing nothing but deep thinking. Thinking about strategies to circumvent the competitors. About ideas to improve our relationship or family life. About delightful ways we could spend the summer. About new products or services that could make us rich. About what we value and where our place is in the world. Et cetera, ad infinitum.

It's important to see the extraordinary cost of this lack of thinking in most people's lives. If we don't think of novel ways out of the challenges we have, we are forced to overcome them purely by working harder, to conquer them by conventional, ordinary means. That's tough work. Long work. Often tedious work. And often unnecessary work—if only we had started thinking before doing.

IDEAS ARE GOLD

One of the greatest ways you can avoid failure in any area of your life is to allocate time every day for serious thinking. Grab your diary now and write in 20 minutes' "Thinking Time" each day for the next week.

Try this for just one week and you will find it transforms your life. Your stress levels will drop as you begin to think through problems you've not fully thought through before. Your effectiveness will sky-rocket as you come up with solutions that will save you hours of work. Your confidence will rise as you begin to feel more in control of the myriad jobs that have been piling up.

Come on, try it—just 20 minutes' thinking time set aside in your diary each day for one week. It won't kill you. Actually, it may keep some of you alive.

When you do this exercise, you may have the same revelation I did. After scheduling thinking time regularly I began to see the incredible importance of good ideas in keeping our whole civilization thriving. Unless we balance working with creating ideas, our progress both personally and as a race will be stunted.

Let's take a look at the world of business as an example. Were all the greatest companies created just by hard work? Well, sure, hard work played a big part. The founders of any successful company were completely dedicated to reaching their goals, no matter how many hours late into the night they had to put in. But the cold hard fact is that there are hundreds of millions of people working very hard and still not creating extraordinary companies. Hard work is not the full answer.

No, what often made big companies big was the quality of the ideas in their first year.

Dell is one of the world's biggest PC companies. Did Michael Dell defeat all his giant competitors by just working more hours than they did? Not at all. Dell grew rapidly as a company because of a single brilliant idea that Michael had when he was in his college dorm. He believed people would like buying computers direct via mail order, rather than through the usual dealers. By buying direct they'd save both time and money. So he started booking ads in computer magazines and within weeks he had a pile of orders—and Dell Computer was born.

Did Starbucks CEO Howard Schultz become a billionaire by working really hard? Well, Schultz is renowned for putting in the hours—but so is anyone who runs one café, let alone several thousand of them. No, it was Howard's great idea that America would love the kind of specialized coffee hangouts that are everywhere in Italy. He came up with the concept of "the third place," a spot between home and work that people could come to chill out, meet friends, and enjoy a break. My point is that it was his core idea that made Starbucks great, not working 20 hours a day.

What about the Body Shop, one of the world's most successful bath and beauty companies? It grew from two very simple ideas. When Anita Roddick opened her first shop she couldn't afford fancy bottles like her competitors. Instead, she packaged everything in the same inexpensive plastic bottles, passing the savings on to her customers. She was also deeply concerned about the livelihoods of the tribal communities she bought her ingredients from, and wanted to make sure they were looked after and supported. This enlightened capitalism became a key part of her brand and gained her millions of dollars' worth of publicity. She began to get great press coverage because her company wasn't just driven by profits: it was propelled by a desire to help the communities that made her ingredients.

Ideas, ideas, ideas. The lifeblood of great companies and the fuel for great lives.

BRAINSTORM REGULARLY

So ponder this: when was the last time you sat down with a blank piece of paper and a pen and just brainstormed some terrific ideas? For your social life, for your health, for your job? For your future?

If it's been more than a week, then I believe you're not doing it frequently enough to maximize your success. For many people, it may have been months or even years since they deliberately brainstormed ideas.

That's the first part of becoming a great thinker—scheduling time for it. The second part is to become an expert at idea-generation methodologies.

IDEA CREATION TECHNIQUES THAT WORK

What techniques do most people use to conceive ideas? The answer is: none. They just sit down and hope something great pops into their head. While that beats doing nothing, imagine how much better the results would be if you had some proven techniques and systems to maximize your creativity. Far superior, I think you'll agree.

I've thought long and hard about this issue because for most of my life I've been a professional idea creator. Working in the creative department in an advertising agency, there was often enormous pressure to conceive brilliant ideas day in and day out. Failure to come up with gems could mean ending up unemployed.

As a result I've spent many hours looking for the most reliable idea-creation techniques. I'd now like to give you some of the best ones I've discovered.

A century ago most people thought creativity was just some God-given skill—you either had it or you didn't. But in the last fifteen years researchers have found that our creativity can be massively boosted—by our diet, by the amount we exercise, by how much sleep we get, and by using specific idea-creation methods.

So if you're one of those people who think you haven't got a creative bone in your body, think again. Anyone (and I mean anyone) can be a creative powerhouse if they just focus on it and use some of the top-level techniques I am about to reveal.

The Dictionary Method

One of the finest idea-cracking methods is called the Dictionary Method. It's a cinch. Just pick a simple word from a dictionary or a magazine or out of your head. Basic words like cat, house, tree, moon, chair, octopus, and so on are best. Now think of your creative problem or challenge. How could you relate that problem to this particular word?

Let's say your company needs to get more clients and the word you've chosen is "octopus." Brainstorm around that word and see if any ideas pop into your head connected to that.

For example, an octopus has eight arms, so maybe eight people in the company could be chosen to make new business phone calls each morning. Or maybe you could send letters, postcards, or gifts to potential clients eight times a year. Or on the eighth day of every month you could invite a room full of prospects in for a glass of wine and to hear a speaker on a subject relevant to their business.

Octopuses live in the sea. Perhaps you could take potential clients out for a great afternoon on a boat. Octopuses release ink, so maybe you could write a personal letter to all the clients you used to work with in the past, asking if they have any projects you can help them with. Octopuses have suction cups on their arms so their prey can't get away. What could you do *after* a big presentation to prevent the clients from choosing another company?

You get the picture.

The really interesting thing about this technique is just how quickly you can come up with relevant ideas to your particular challenge (for example, the ideas I just presented to you were conceived in under two minutes). If I'd chosen another word to brainstorm with, let's say "chicken," I would have come up with an entirely different set of ideas. Each word directs your mind in different directions.

Just think of the potential power of this method. If you did this process with five or six words, one after another, in the space of half an hour you would have a huge array of new, lateral solutions to whatever problem you happen to be faced with.

Be patient with it, though. It may take a while before you get used to the methodology. But once you've learned it, you've learned it for life. The Dictionary Method alone used for just 10 minutes daily has the capacity to transform your business and personal life.

The Ridiculous Idea Method

With this technique you think of crazy solutions, absurd ideas, outlandish concepts, then try to see if any ideas stem from them.

Here's an example. Imagine that you own an accounting firm and you want to double the number of clients you have. How could you do it? Well, let's think of some crazy, wild ideas and see what good ideas come from them.

Outrageous idea 1: We could get more clients by closing our company. What an absurd idea. But does it lead to a useful idea? Well, maybe if you closed your business every Friday and spent the whole day generating new business you could get some big results.

Outrageous idea 2: We could get more business by not charging any money for our services. Madness! But hold on, maybe you could be the first accountancy firm to give a money-back guarantee. If clients don't think you're courteous, professional, and expert you'll refund your fees. That idea would probably entice some new clients to give the firm a go.

Outrageous idea 3: We could increase our clients if we were rude to them. Now that's the dumbest idea in the world, but how could you create something useful from the concept? Well, maybe you could introduce a service that warns clients when the fundamentals of their business are off course. These could be called "We Don't Mean to Be Rude, But . . . " sessions. In these meetings clients would be given honest, frank, hard-core (and maybe even a little rude) counseling on how and why they need to get their business on track.

Outrageous idea 4: We'd get more clients by tripling our prices. Seems a pretty stupid concept, huh? Well, not so fast. Perhaps you could introduce a special high-priced service where you're available 24/7. Or other clients get the opportunity to come to special entrepreneurs' dinners monthly. Or customers get to meet the world's top investment advisers whenever they're in town. Or clients at this elite level are given investment tips no one else usually gets.

As you can see, coming up with insane ideas and then thinking about how you could make them work is actually a surprisingly effective way to generate unique solutions. This technique puts your mind in an unusual place. It forces you to think in ways you may never have thought before. Because you're attacking the problem from such a strange angle, the concepts you generate are often far more creative than those that come from standard brainstorming sessions.

When was the last time you had a really outlandish idea? Something totally off the wall? Maybe it's time you pushed your imagination to the outer edges. Who knows—you could come up with some absolute gems.

The Ridiculous Idea Method is particularly good for situations when everybody involved is in a creative rut, such as in companies that have been doing things the same way for years, or that are too slow-moving and conservative. It's a mental wake-up call, a mind shape-up. Done at the right time, its effect can be absolutely revolutionary.

The Different Industry Method

If you can't come up with your own ideas, steal them!

What a fantastic methodology this is. It's a wonderful way to come up with totally new ideas for your business, simply by taking them from other industries. You'll be absolutely astonished at how many industries that appear to be completely different from yours actually use systems, procedures, and techniques that would be perfect for your business.

Let me tell you an interesting story. A few years ago I was giving a speech on high performance at a real-estate agents' seminar in New Zealand. As I knew little about the property-selling industry I decided that rather than just working in my hotel room I would watch the other speakers.

Wow, did I ever get an awakening.

I heard method after method of acquiring customers that nobody in my industry—the advertising world—had ever been taught. Smart ideas for cold-calling prospects, how to structure sales presentations, systems for following up potential clients, advanced time-management techniques, sophisticated delegation methods, and so on. These real-estate guys were absolute masters at selling stuff!

Many of their ideas were applicable to my industry but I knew they weren't being used by my competitors. As soon as I landed in my home-town I implemented the best of the ideas and my results improved immediately. And I've been using many of these clever strategies ever since.

So here's an important question for you: what could you learn from another industry? What could a lawyer teach you about negotiations? What could a surgeon teach you about stress relief? What could an insurance salesperson teach you about time manage-ment? What could a direct-mail company teach you about client retention?

Here's how to improve your results within the next week with this idea. Take five minutes now to think of 10 friends of yours who work in an industry different from yours. Write their names down on a piece of paper. Now, looking at that list, which three do you think could teach you stuff about how they work that might really help you?

OK—got the three finalists? Good. Phone all three in the next 10 minutes and set up a coffee meeting or lunch to get their best hints on how their business systems could help yours. It's 10 minutes that could revolutionize your results in the next year.

And if you're not in business, be assured that the Different Industry Method can still work for you. If you're a homemaker, you can learn some very powerful strategies from the restaurant industry, the account-ing business, the kindergarten world, even the therapy business, on how to improve life at home.

If you're a student, think about what wisdom you could collect from business productivity experts, the nutrition industry, the computing world, or professional public speakers to help you get higher academic marks.

Or if you're a pro athlete, what could you learn from the sales promotions business, the massage therapists' association, the travel industry, or the book publishing folks?

Please think deeply about this. The fact is, this one technique alone can dramatically elevate your achievement levels if you apply it regularly and consistently.

After all, it's damn hard getting ahead of the pack when you're just doing the same things as everyone else. Find yourself a different strategy from a different industry and it's conceivable that you will quite literally be the only person in your entire sector using that technique. If it's a half-decent technique, you're going to enjoy a major advantage over your competition.

The Star Emulation Method

Next up is an interesting psychological strategy that I've found highly useful when I'm stuck in a thinking rut. Like me, you've probably experienced times when you just can't seem to come up with a solution to a problem. Your ideas are the same as everyone else's and frankly the problem appears unsolvable.

Well, perhaps it's unsolvable by you, but what if the president of the United States had to solve it? Or Bill Gates? What solution would a famous heavy-metal rocker come up with? Or a professional poker player? If your boss walked into the room, what kind of solutions do you think he or she would suggest? What about your mother—how do you imagine she would solve the problem?

Now obviously I'm not suggesting you actually ask these people (although if you've got a direct line to the White House, heck, give it a shot!). I'm recommending that you just imagine for 10 minutes that you are one of these individuals. Put yourself in their shoes, behave like them, try to guess how they would think if faced with the very same challenge you have.

It may seem a little strange to you at first, but I have used this technique many times when I've faced a difficult situation, or when I've simply been thinking about a problem for so long that my answers have become predictable and stale.

When I was a full-time advertising writer I would often think of the great British or American ad writers and pretend they were working on the ad campaign, not me. If I wanted to do a more playful concept I would pretend I was a particular top Brazilian advertising creator, and if I was aiming to do or create something highly artistic I would sometimes imagine I was one of Tokyo's top advertising designers. (It helped if I studied their work beforehand, or read a few pages of something they'd written to help put me in the mood.)

In almost every case I found that within half an hour I had a pile of ideas that were fresher, more original, and often more appropriate than those I had been creating previously.

The method can be used if you're a parent at home, too. Ask yourself what ideas Martha Stewart might come up with for an upcoming dinner party? How would Oprah solve this family argument? You get the picture.

The Star Emulation Method is a smart way to force your mind to think in new, more lateral ways. When you first start using the method it will probably feel a little odd, but stick with it and I'm certain you'll get lasting value and a mountain of clever solutions using it.

The Famous Method

Finally, we come to the fifth idea-creation method: the Famous Method. With this technique you simply ask yourself one powerful question: how could I come up with a solution to this problem that would actually make me (or my company) famous?

You don't get famous doing ordinary things—you have to do something amazing, even outlandish, to get the media knocking on your door.

What could it be? I love this strategy because it makes you think really big thoughts, far bigger than your mind would usually come up with.

Imagine the TV news crews coming to your office or home begging for an interview because of the amazing way you handled a problem or challenge. Maybe it's a hilarious solution. Or a publicity-seeking solution. Perhaps you involved the services of a famous Hollywood personality, an animal, or some cute kids. Think hard. What is a solution so special, so extraordinary, that the media would view it as something worth featuring in a magazine or newspaper, on a news website or on TV?

I'm not saying this idea-generating technique is easy, but I do think you'll have loads of fun brainstorming some crazy solutions. Who knows—somewhere among that list of zany ideas could be a piece of sheer genius.

CREATIVITY REWARDS EFFORT

Which leads me to one of the most important aspects of idea creating: make sure you come up with lots and lots of ideas, not just a handful. Most people don't come up with nearly enough ideas when they're creating; they usually just come up with four or five and pick the best one of those. But the world's most creative people understand that to consistently come up with fantastic ideas you have to conceive lots of dull, ordinary, even terrible ideas first.

When I was working in advertising I would often come up with hundreds of ideas for each advertisement. By thinking up so many it was almost inevitable that at least a few would be good. As in any other area of life, creativity rewards effort. At the very minimum, you should set yourself the goal of coming up with 10 ideas every time you need one idea. Doing that alone will make a huge difference to the quality (and quantity) of your ideas output.

TIME FOR PRACTICE

Now you have something probably none of your competitors have: a storehouse of powerful methodologies that can make you one of the most creative and therefore most successful people around. Start to use these techniques and your peers will be shocked at the quality of the solutions you regularly put forward. You will become a mighty idea-generation machine.

You can use these methods for problems at home, in your personal life—in fact, in any area where you feel stuck for fresh solutions.

Now you've got this powerful arsenal of techniques it's up to you to use them frequently. A good way to do this is to schedule a time each week, let's say Friday afternoon, where you reserve 20 minutes just for idea generation. Write it in your diary and it's much more likely to happen. Do this one thing and you will increase the time you spend generating ideas by a factor of 10 or more.

And I don't care how "uncreative" you think you are—if you're spending 20 minutes a week generating ideas using the methods in this chapter, you're going to come up with at least a few truly great ideas to improve your income and indeed your life.

no daily rituals

When I walk into my local gym I see a huge poster with some of the wisest words ever written: Inspiration gets you started, habit keeps you going.

That is so true! Not just for exercising, but for success in any field at all. Let's be honest: we've all started a project with immense enthusiasm and vigor only to find a few weeks later that we've run out of motivation and can hardly bring ourselves to keep working on it. As the Bible puts it, "The spirit is willing but the flesh is weak."

For years I used to beat myself up about giving up on cherished projects, until one day I got a bit smarter and started asking myself why this occurred.

I think there are two basic reasons. The first is purely mental: we start linking more pain to moving forward on a project, and more pleasure to not working on it. It's all about neural associations. When once you thought about the project as exciting, your brain now sees it as drudgery and tedium to do even an hour's work on it. In your mind, the glamour has gone.

However, there's another reason that enables even average people to become champions of life and ultimately outperform others who seemingly have more talent. It's a facet of success rarely talked about, yet it is very possibly the number one determinant of whether you will succeed or fail in any major undertaking.

That, my friends, is the awesome power of Daily Rituals. As that poster in my gym emphasizes, it's what you get into the habit of doing that keeps you going, long after the initial excitement of your goals has faded.

That's why it's so important to keep thinking about all the good things that will occur when you reach your intended goal. By forcing yourself to constantly think about the ultimate victory ahead, you remain inspired to continue down the path to get there. As the great philosopher Nietszche famously put it, "He who has a why to live for can bear almost any how."

If you examine your thinking patterns when you give up on something or lack powerful motivation to keep going, I think you'll find that you're spending a lot of time thinking about how unpleasant taking the steps to your goal are, rather than the glory of achieving the goal itself. Big mistake.

Our quality of life is largely determined by the direction of our thinking. Thinking constantly about the outcome is always more inspiring than contemplating the process—which, let's be honest, is often boring.

The somewhat ugly truth about success is that it consists of lots of small, often tedious steps. Expect excitement all the way to your goal and you'll surely be disappointed. The bigger the goal, the more boring steps you'll have to take. Simple.

I think it's important that people recognize this. If everyone understood this critical aspect of success when it occurred in their lives, they would be much less likely to give up when the going got tough.

We see elite athletes surrounded by paparazzi as they walk into a televised awards ceremony and we think we want their life. But so often the day after that glamorous event you'll find them back at the track, vomiting from the hardships of training (they don't like to show that part on primetime TV), or rising at 4:30 AM to do two hours of laps in a lonely pool, or lifting weights until their muscles fail because they're utterly exhausted.

How do athletes keep going under such arduous conditions? They keep their eyes and minds focused on the prize, rather than on the current pain they're experiencing.

THE MIRACLE OF RITUALS

If you can add a structure to your goals, a ritual you do daily, you will increase the chances of achieving them by 1,000 percent. Believe me, I have tested this concept for decades. When I created a goal and didn't have a daily program or ritual of steps I had to follow to reach it, I often floundered, became inefficient, and ultimately gave up. But when I created a ritual for myself, I found it much easier to get up in the morning, follow my program, and achieve progress towards my dream.

Rituals work. Rituals are vital to your future success, no matter what area you play in. The simple reality is that if you're not achieving all that you'd like in life, it's probably because you haven't established a daily ritual and written it in your diary. Daily rituals are that important.

Look at the self-help section of the bookshop, or at all those high-energy, fist-pumping motivation seminars held around the world. There's often great material in those books and at those conferences, but a few weeks after you've read the latest self-help genius's book or attended the seminar, you're back doing the same old stuff.

Why? Habit. It's both humanity's curse and our greatest opportunity. If we can just get into the right positive habits, we can make fantastic progress. But if we just rely on inspiration, it's virtually inevitable that we'll slip back into the old ways of doing things as soon as that first burst of inspiration has departed.

A SYSTEM CAN HELP YOU
ACHIEVE YOUR GOALS

What daily rituals do you have? What systems do you use that guide you, support you, and help you every day to create the life you desire to live?

Sadly, most people have no positive daily rituals. They get up, trudge to work, go home and watch TV on the sofa until they nod off to sleep. Then the next day they get up and do it all over again.

Sure, some do a bit of daily exercise or read some positive books, which is certainly a good start, but there are precious few people who have developed powerful daily rituals both at home and at work that give them the support they need to consistently achieve at a high level. It would make all the difference if they did.

Consider this. If you had a success ritual you practiced each day that consisted of three intelligent steps or actions, then by the end of the year you would have taken well over 1,000 steps towards your goals. An extraordinary accomplishment! Yet it was only three actions daily.

It's a bit like the miracle of compound interest, which financial advisers often talk about. When you make a small amount of profit each year but reinvest it the next year, it accumulates rapidly and exponentially. Within five years you have grown an astonishingly large financial nest egg.

There is an ancient story about a man who did a favor for a king. The king sought to reward the man highly. The man said all he wanted was for the king to put a single grain of rice on one square of a chessboard. On the next square he wanted two grains of rice, and so on, each square doubling the previous amount. Sounds like a pretty humble request, right? Well, do the math. By the time he got to the last square of the chessboard, the king would have owed the man millions of grains of rice!

That's the power of compounding. It's similar to the power of the daily ritual. A few steps each day can lead to momentous progress down the track.

I can honestly say that the practice of daily rituals has changed my life. When I follow specific rituals each day, I am sometimes astounded at the progress I make. I can't emphasize this enough. If you read this book and don't establish at least one daily ritual to help you put the ideas into practice, I believe the chances of your improving significantly are small. But if you create at least a few key rituals, you will make real progress.

Now let's get to work.

SEVEN EXCELLENT RITUALS

What follows are a series of rituals designed to support you in achieving all kinds of goals. All you have to do is pick which ritual system fits your aims and create a copy of it to post in several places where you'll see it (perhaps on your bathroom mirror and near your computer at work).

Then, when you awaken each morning, make the promise to yourself that whatever happens that day you will complete your success ritual. No matter what.

At first it may feel unnatural or inhibiting to have to follow a daily ritual, but stick with it for a couple of weeks and it will begin to become a habit. Once you get that habitual momentum, there'll be no stopping you. You'll be on the fast track to high achievement.

As you view the rituals I've created in the next few pages, feel free to change them to fit your precise needs and goals. Use them as a basic framework but tailor them to suit you ideally.

Industry Mastery Ritual

This ritual is for people who want to become renowned experts in their field. To be known as the best in your industry means you have to keep up with the latest industry trends and push yourself to keep learning daily. As long as you devote 30 minutes each day to industry mastery, within just one year I guarantee your coworkers will consider you an absolute expert in your field.

> **INDUSTRY MASTERY RITUAL**
>
> **Daily**
> - Read an industry book (20 minutes)
> - Read industry magazines, websites, and blogs (10 minutes)
>
> **Quarterly**
> - Have coffee with one industry expert
>
> **Annually**
> - Attend two industry conferences

That's all there is to it. Just follow this simple ritual and your career is likely to skyrocket. Soon you really will know more about your field than almost everyone in the country.

Anti-Procrastination Ritual

Do you suffer from procrastination? I sure do. I've developed a system that helps eliminate or at least dramatically reduce how often I procrastinate on important tasks. Follow each simple step and watch how much more you achieve. The keys to beating procrastination are getting absolutely clear about what you need to do, setting priorities, and then doing the most valuable tasks first.

> **ANTI-PROCRASTINATION RITUAL**
>
> **Morning**
> - Visualize your goals are achieved (10 minutes)
> - Write today's to-do list
> - Choose the top two most important goals on the list
> - Begin immediately on the first one
> - Spend 10 minutes or more on each of your other key tasks

The program is simple but gets results fast. By forcing yourself to get clear on your day's activities, you'll immediately increase you motivation to do the work. By getting into the habit of starting on your most important tasks first, you'll get fast momentum and progress. Then, by devoting a mere 10 minutes to the other tasks, you'll at least move them forward. (If you want to spend more than 10 minutes on a task, go ahead, but by limiting it to 10 minutes it's easy to get it done and not procrastinate about it.) I use this system regularly and it works.

Social Life Improvement Ritual

Anything can be quickly and easily improved with the right daily ritual—even your social life. If you want more fun with more friends, don't just leave it to chance. Make it happen with the following effective ritual.

SOCIAL LIFE IMPROVEMENT RITUAL
- Make a list of the friends and acquaintances you'd like to see more often
- Read the list each morning
- Set a target of one social event including one of these people each week (coffee, lunch, movie, and so on)
- Make one call or e-mail each day to say hello or to arrange a get-together with friends

The trick with this ritual is the one call or e-mail a day to your friends and acquaintances. Within a short period of time you'll have three weekly social appointments, I assure you. After you've got your three, arrange some for the following weeks or just contact people to say hello.

The cool thing about the Social Life Improvement Ritual is that it can be completed in just 10 minutes a day.

Goal Achievement Ritual

Got something you've wanted to get done for ages, but never seem to make progress on it? Hey, join the club. Millions of people have numerous ideas they just never quite get around to starting on, let alone completing. What you need is a simple ritual that at least ensures that you make daily progress on your goal.

Once you get things moving and you see yourself progressing toward the goal, your enthusiasm will dramatically improve and you'll find it much easier to do more work on the task.

If you haven't made progress on your goal it's normally because of one of two things:

1. *You link something bad to working on or achieving your goal* (it's a lot of work, life will become too different if you achieve it, you'll have to move to another city, your friends may laugh at you, and so forth).
2. *You don't have a daily program to take steps towards the goal.* You get busy with all the other stuff life throws at you, then suddenly realize another month has gone by without you moving any closer to your real dream.

Never fear, this ritual deals with both issues.

GOAL ACHIEVEMENT RITUAL

- Visualize your goal achieved three times a day
- Put up reminder notes reminding you of your goal
- Break your goal down into smaller steps
- Set a deadline for each step
- Read your goals list each morning before work
- Use your diary to set time daily to work on your goal

Perhaps the most important step in this ritual is the last one. When you actually allocate time in your diary to working on a goal, you will inevitably make progress on it. You have to treat that goal as something important, clearly scheduled and that can't be missed. You don't have to spend hours on your goal—30 minutes will often do—but make sure it's an unbreakable appointment with yourself. Just watch what happens.

Ideally make it the same time each day. Let those around you know that your ritual is compulsory and unchangeable and pretty soon they'll get used to it and know to leave you alone for that period. Be firm with them. Until you start treating that goal seriously, nobody else will.

Clean Home Ritual

Wow, did I ever need this one! I used to be a complete home slob. My place was a mess. Sometimes it took me 20 minutes just to find my car keys. But by following a basic ritual each day I now find it easy to keep my hacienda clean and neat. If you walked around my apartment now, you would never guess I used to be messy and disorganized—the place is in great order. All it took was this three-step ritual.

CLEAN HOME RITUAL

Before work
- 10-minute clean-up of home

Before bed
- 10-minute clean-up of home

Every Saturday
- Do laundry; throw out unneeded items (10 minutes)

That's it! Pretty basic, yes, but it works like a charm. It becomes a habit really quickly and within 10 days it feels completely effortless. In fact, I often enjoy doing it (no, really!). Believe me, you get a good feeling when you start arriving home to an ever-cleaner place, and it's absolutely amazing how much cleaning you can do in just 10 minutes, especially when it's each and every day. After about two weeks you'll find your house is already basically clean even before you start your morning clean-up. Resist the urge to miss a day! Look for things to clean or throw out that you don't normally look at, such as old books, clothes, cupboards, and so on.

If you wait until your place is messy before you do the cleaning, it will not develop into a habit. Absolute consistency is the key. Build up that daily habit so that it's totally automatic, so that it takes little effort and virtually no willpower. You may find it hard to believe that cleaning your home could ever be effortless, but trust me—when you do it habitually each and every day, 10 minutes in the morning and 10 minutes in the evening, it becomes dead easy.

The last point in the ritual is an important one. I've found that if you throw out one or two items of old clothing, books, or unnecessary items each week, your place quickly looks neater and tidier. It also makes things vastly easier to find.

Happiness Ritual

In the last fifteen years there has been a colossal amount of research conducted on what makes humans happy (I'll reveal some of the latest findings in Chapter Fifteen). Suffice to say that there are numerous things you can do to quickly improve your mood.

Let's face it: nobody feels fantastic every day. We all have our dark periods. But by following this elementary yet exceedingly potent ritual, you can tangibly reduce your black moods and enjoy vastly greater periods of feeling happy.

The important point to remember about happiness is that it is not just dependent on events that occur in your life. It is your *reaction* to those events that dictates your mood. If you choose to just shrug your shoulders and brush off adversity, then bad moments won't hurt you much. If you become a drama queen and take bad stuff personally, regular stress and misery will be your companions. Ultimately it really is up to you. The moment you take responsibility for your moods, you begin to see that you are in control of them. It's a very important mental game you must learn to play.

Make this ritual of mood control part of your life and just watch how your moods improve.

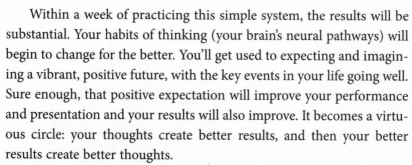

HAPPINESS RITUAL

Early morning
- Visualize the day going well (5 minutes)
- List all the good things in your life
- Exercise (10 minutes plus)

Evening
- Review all the good moments of the day (1 minute)
- Think of all the things you're grateful for (1 minute)
- Visualize your life going well (5 minutes)

Within a week of practicing this simple system, the results will be substantial. Your habits of thinking (your brain's neural pathways) will begin to change for the better. You'll get used to expecting and imagining a vibrant, positive future, with the key events in your life going well. Sure enough, that positive expectation will improve your performance and presentation and your results will also improve. It becomes a virtuous circle: your thoughts create better results, and then your better results create better thoughts.

Now consider the alternative. If you don't do this daily happiness ritual, your moods are far more likely to go up and down with your changing circumstances. People who don't have a system for regulating their moods experience more oscillations in their happiness. Without a controlling force, they are virtually certain to sail on rougher mental waters.

In my opinion, this ritual is one of the most important features of this book. I can think of no more valuable technique to quickly improve the quality of your daily experience and uplift the level of your thinking.

After all, why is it that so many people want to be rich, successful, or famous? It's because of the way they believe it will make them *feel*. Well, rather than spend years trying to reach those goals, why not be more direct and simply address your moods themselves? Do the Happiness Ritual each day and you'll feel great. In fact, you'll feel better than many people who are rich or famous actually feel day to day. To master your moods is truly to be king of the world.

The next ritual is equally simple, but also highly important for those who seek to develop a better quality of life.

Fitness Ritual

Of course, there are hundreds of ways to keep fit, healthy, and vibrant, but if you've had trouble sticking to a fitness regime, try this system. I've developed it with several principles in mind.

The first is that it's better to do even a bit of exercise daily than none. Even when you work out just a little, your blood flows better, your lymph recirculates, your hormone balance is readjusted, and your body and brain become better oxygenated. Equally important, you feel encouraged that you got some exercise done, so your self-esteem increases.

The second principle behind the Fitness Ritual is that once you get used to doing just a small amount of exercise daily, it's much more likely that you will soon extend your exercise period.

The third principle is all about minimizing effort. I believe that one of the main reasons people give up exercising is that they view it as painful. This is often the fault of personal trainers. In an attempt to get their clients fit fast, they work them into the ground. Pretty soon the clients dread going to the gym—it's just too darn hard. When your mind starts seeing exercise in this way, it takes absolute iron willpower not to call it quits. Few are that strong.

So frankly, I'm an advocate of regular daily exercise as long as it's pleasant, with only occasional attempts to push yourself. I'm well aware that this strategy is unlikely to lead to extraordinarily quick fitness gains, but it will ensure that you are far less likely to give up after just a few workouts. For most people, working out moderately but regularly is a more effective strategy than exercising hard for a month or two and then giving up.

That's what this Fitness Ritual is all about: regularity, enjoyment, and consistency, all in just a few minutes a day.

The reason I include visualization in the program is that one of the main barriers to a nonexerciser getting fit is their self-image—they see themselves as unfit. I totally believe that the key to lasting change (in any area of life) is to first create a new picture in your mind of how you want to be and then keep thinking about that picture. Within weeks you usually start behaving more in accordance with that vision.

If you begin a fitness program but still see yourself as an unfit, overweight pig, then it's highly unlikely you'll maintain your program. The thought of being a regular exerciser simply won't match how you envision yourself, and you'll give up the workouts.

This is the problem with many diets. Sure, they address the physical aspect of dieting (reducing fat, counting calories, and so on), but until the internal mental picture of yourself (your self-projection) is that of someone getting fitter and slimmer, then the only thing that will be slim is your chances of sticking with the program.

Here's the Fitness Ritual, to be performed seven days a week.

FITNESS RITUAL

Early morning
- 10 minutes visualizing yourself fit, slim, and in love with exercising (visualize to inspiring music)
- 15 minutes fast walking, jogging, or exercising

Evening
- 5 minutes visualizing as per morning

Now remember, this is a program for people who just can't bring themselves to train regularly, so it's deliberately easy. But I can assure you, if all you do is 15 minutes of fast walking seven days a week, you will see some amazing changes in your body shape and energy levels.

Keep it short and sharp and you'll have little trouble doing it every day. But do it at the same time every day—this will help ingrain it as a habit. If you miss a morning, then have an alternative time at midday or in the evening that you automatically switch to. That way, if you miss the workout you immediately switch to Plan B later in the day.

Performing rituals at precisely the same time each day really helps them become a habit and makes the process as automatic as possible. The less you have to think about it, the more easily you'll just do it. If you have a different training time each day, it's twice as hard to transform it into a habit.

JUST PICK THREE

Truly, if you create three rituals in your life—one for exercise, one for your work day, and maybe one to maximize your recreation time—you will vastly improve the quality of your life. But if you don't have rituals, your progress in any area will be slower and more haphazard.

Rituals are the real secret to success. They are the difference between performing averagely and performing superbly over the medium and long term. Look at people successful in their field and I guarantee they will have tasks and procedures they do day in and day out without fail.

If you're not getting the results you desire, in any area of your life, it's almost certain a lack of ritual is the culprit. Develop a simple daily program and stick to it, and in a few weeks you'll have reset the compass of your life and be well on your way to excellence again. It doesn't have to be an elaborate ritual, or even particularly time-consuming; it just has to be consistent.

Better a few minutes each day working on a goal than no time at all or only occasional effort. Your momentum will build, your enthusiasm will rise, and you'll soon become a dynamic, powerful, peak performer. Little by little, you'll be creating the life of your dreams.

That's the awesome power of rituals.

stress

What a killer stress is.

A killer of dreams. A killer of happiness. And in the end a killer of people as well. Increasingly, medical researchers believe that stress plays a crucial role in weakening our immune system and thereby shortening our lifespan. Make no mistake: if you view your life as stressful, you are putting your very existence at risk.

Now, if you're in your twenties or thirties, your body can probably handle the stress. But if you are aged 40 or above, you are really rolling the dice if you are regularly in the stress zone.

Here's an amazing statistic. Have a guess what time of the week most heart attacks occur. Give up? Around 9 AM on Monday! Why? Probably because people are really worried about their upcoming day. In a nutshell, they're totally stressed.

Interestingly, most people in today's society just accept stress. They see it as an inevitable part of life in the modern world. And yes, it's true: some degree of stress is assured in our fast-paced, deadline-oriented existence. But be careful. You may be underestimating the level of stress you now have. You may in fact be so used to being in a highly stressed state that you view your condition as normal.

I remember going for a vacation on the idyllic island of Boracay in the Philippines. I was there at least five days before I truly began to relax. Only after that time, as my body and mind slowed down and became really rejuvenated, did I finally see clearly how stressed I had actually been. Before that time I had no idea how stressed I was. What I took to be a normal lifestyle I eventually realized was a highly stressed one.

Maybe you are the same. Perhaps you are just used to being stressed out. So let's put it to the test to find out how stressed you really are. Take a minute to answer the following questions.

Stress Indication Quiz

	YES	NO
I often wake up tired		
I often have trouble getting to sleep		
I feel overwhelmed by my workload		
I sometimes snap at others		
I frequently breathe out in exasperation		
I am an overthinker		
I rarely have time to exercise		
I eat at irregular times		
I have more than two coffees most days		
I suspect my sex drive is below average		
I have a headache at least once a month		
I swallow my food without chewing it properly		
I work more than 10 hours a day		
I haven't had a vacation for more than a year		
I need alcohol to wind down each evening		

How'd you do?

If you answered yes to seven or more questions I'd put you in the Danger category. As many studies show that stress is one of the leading causes of disease and death, this is simply not acceptable. You need to change.

This book is about the causes of failure, and surely there is no greater failure than dying decades before you should because you didn't manage your stress levels. But even assuming your life is not threatened by stress (and that's a big assumption), let's take a look at some of the other insidious ways that stress contributes to life failure.

STRESS AFFECTS PERFORMANCE

When you're stressed it's hard to keep working at a high level. You get tired more easily, frustrated more often. You're far more likely to make impulsive, rash decisions that will prove to be foolish down the track. When you're stressed your concentration wavers and your ability to take in large amounts of data weakens. You often perform at a level below that normally expected of a person of your intelligence and experience.

STRESS AFFECTS RELATIONSHIPS

In many ways your success or failure in life is dependent on the quality of your relationships with people, both at work and socially. As Dr. Daniel Goleman showed with his work on emotional intelligence, when you get along with people you get ahead, in your work life and your personal life. There's a direct correlation with the way you treat others and the level of stress you're experiencing. Haven't we all regretted reacting angrily to someone when we've been stressed? When you're constantly stressed out you become a lower-quality, more primitive, less accommodating version of yourself. It can be ugly to watch. Many times a single angry reaction to someone (often caused primarily by stress) can ruin a relationship for years or even decades. It's a bitter price to pay.

STRESS INHIBITS YOUR SEX LIFE

Stress affects your performance in the bedroom as much as in the boardroom. Both men and women report a lower sex drive when they are stressed out. Often the only thing they're interested in when they get into bed is sleep, so exhausted are they by their workload and mental burdens. It's hardly surprising. The human body puts a priority on survival above procreation, so if you're feeling highly stressed, your body will not be encouraging you to get amorous—it just wants to get well again. Even if you do end up having sex, it will usually be a pretty average experience if you're mentally exhausted. If stress is a regular occurrence in your life then it's not hard to see how a relationship can become strained after just a few months.

STRESS AFFECTS YOUR PROFITS

Nobody likes dealing with someone who is stressed. Clearly if a client's or customer's common experience of you is that you're agitated, frustrated, or irritated, they're going to take their business elsewhere. People underestimate the importance of giving customers an upbeat experience every time they interact with them. In a world where there is a surplus of options, where frankly there are almost too many good choices of which company to buy from, niceness matters.

I have spent most of my life in the advertising industry. Frequently when we pitched an account the client would be spending more than $5 million a year. You would think that with that kind of money at stake, the decision would be made on hard fundamentals like price, product, quality, and so on. But my experience has been the opposite. Countless times I found that the company that won the account was the company the client most enjoyed hanging out with. They reasoned that any of the ad agencies they had shortlisted could do the job, but who would they actually enjoy working with? It all came down to people chemistry.

Now imagine that one of those agencies presenting was full of stressed people. What would their chances be of being awarded the business? Pretty slim, I reckon.

Look at your own performance. Are you coming across as stressed to your clients or friends? If you suspect the answer is yes, then you can bet they're not having a whole lot of fun being around you. They may not say it, but I imagine they are feeling it. The simple fact is that stressed people make less money than relaxed people.

STRESS AFFECTS EVERY ASPECT OF YOUR LIFE

Let's summarize the hazards of stress. It:

Makes you sick
Probably shortens your life
Probably restricts your decision-making capacity
Makes you unhappy
Makes you lose business
Decreases the quality of your social life
Makes you a bad lover
Makes you earn less money
Makes people not want to be around you
Reduces your concentration
Increases your agitation

Wow! That is some list. Is it possible that you are not treating stress as seriously as you should? After all, as we've just seen, it pretty much affects every area of your life.

But never fear—help is at hand. I've spent decades studying stress reduction and I now want to give you a whole heap of techniques I use to keep my stress at low levels. If you suffer from stress, my suggestion is that you pick three of the following solutions and make them a part of your life.

STRESS RELIEVERS

Deep Breathing

Here's a fascinating thing to observe: your breathing patterns change with your moods. When you're angry your breath is often shallower (you may even breathe in short bursts). When you're creating or brainstorming you will often hold your breath as you think deeply. When you're calm your breath is even and deeper.

Our moods fundamentally affect our breathing patterns. But the really interesting point is that it works the other way around, too. When you make the effort to change your breathing style your mood will usually change as well.

So next time you're feeling totally overwhelmed by the world, take five minutes to just go somewhere quiet and breathe deeply. As you exhale, imagine all the stress leaving your body and mind. Then, as you inhale, imagine that a wave of calm, peace, and optimism is entering you. I promise you that if you try this technique you'll be surprised by how quickly it uplifts and relaxes you. We become how we breathe. So train yourself to observe your own breathing, and when life gets stressful, take a moment to adjust it.

By the way, you don't have to be stressed to the max to get value from this technique. If you do five minutes of deep breathing soon after you awake each morning, within a week you'll feel more energized, happier, and definitely more relaxed.

Releasing

If you compare your stress levels in the morning and then in the evening you will usually find the level has increased as the day has gone on. That's pretty normal. Look further into what precisely caused that heightening of stress and you can usually pinpoint 3–5 events or situations that occurred during the day that lifted your agitation level a little. Each event by itself may not have been that bad, but together they caused the stress to mount up.

There's a startlingly simple way to alleviate such tension. Just release the stress several times during the day.

This releasing strategy was perfected by Lester Levenson and Hale Dwoskin over a thirty-year period with a technique known as the Sedona Method. I heartily recommend it. At the core of the Sedona system is the realization that the average person holds their stress inside, rarely letting it go. By getting into the habit of holding their stress in for days, weeks, months, or even decades, it is almost inevitable that their life will eventually be saturated with tension.

Levenson and Dwoskin argue that there are three ways to handle stress. The first two are very common: suppression and expression. With suppression we stay quiet about issues that upset us, rarely letting our true feelings be known—not a strategy likely to lead to ongoing good mental health. But expression has its dangers too. Sure, we often feel better for having expressed our emotions honestly and directly, but often this frankness of expression makes the people we're talking to feel hurt, embarrassed, shocked, or offended, sometimes for a long time afterwards.

Levenson and Dwoskin found that there is a third alternative, rarely practiced but usually more effective than either suppression or expression. They call it releasing. In essence, it's allowing yourself to identify what you're feeling, then letting it leave you.

I won't go into the Sedona Method in detail, but know that it has helped many tens of thousands of people combat their stress quickly and easily. It's worth checking it out at www.sedona.com.

You don't have to do the full Sedona course to benefit from the concept. Just train yourself to release your stress throughout the day. Whenever something (or someone) gets to you, close your eyes, breathe in, and imagine you are letting that frustration and tension go. Just visualize it leaving your body. Do this throughout the day and sure enough, by the end of the afternoon you will feel much more relaxed.

When you release stress regularly, it's far harder for it to build up.

List Making

I know it's a bit strange to suggest that list making will reduce your stress, but it definitely does. I have always found that when I write lists of (a) what I need to do, (b) what my values are, and (c) where I want to go in life, it calms me in a major way.

I think there are several reasons why listing what you need to get done (for the day or for your life) reduces stress. The first is that making a list gives you a sense of order, helping you feel that you're in control of your life. And as many cognitive behavior therapists will tell you, when you feel you are in control you're much more likely to feel happy.

The second reason why making to-do lists reduces your angst is that it gets rid of a lot of greyness and uncertainty in your life. Often when you feel stressed it's not just because you have a lot of stuff to do, it's because you're not exactly sure of all the things you need to get done. You have a sneaking feeling that you've forgotten about something important, that you're going to drop the ball and miss something vital. That obviously is going to cause stress.

But when you take half an hour to write not just a to-do list but a comprehensive series of lists for every area of your life, then you rest easy. As organizational guru David Allen has proved, your brain can handle having heaps of things undone so long as it knows what they are.

I suggest you get a blank notebook and create a page for each of these life categories:

Work
Personal
Finance
Calls
Follow-up
One day (this is where you list all the non-urgent stuff you'll get around
    to one day)

Then write down all the tasks you have to do in each of these areas.

In addition to this I suggest a page for the traditional daily to-do list. Take the most immediate and important tasks from your other lists and put them on that daily to-do list each morning before you start your work day.

Are all these lists necessary? I think so, yes. Although it may seem like overkill, you will soon feel terrific knowing that you well and truly have every aspect of your life covered. It's a tremendous stress reliever.

The Circle of Influence

When you really feel overwhelmed with stuff to handle, spilt your tasks and issues into two categories and write each list inside a circle. In the first circle put all the challenges you can do little about (fears about the economy, what someone else may do, things other people need to handle, and the like). In the second circle list all the things you can actually change and improve—any situations or tasks you can act on. This is your Circle of Influence.

Too many people fret about stuff they can't really change. It's useless, futile, and totally unproductive. If, however, you can discipline yourself to purely focus on the tasks where you can actually make a difference, then you are sure to improve your life. If you have to worry, at least worry about the things you have the power to change.

The Circle of Influence exercise is a wonderful way to reduce stress because it instantly halves your immediate workload and your list of active concerns. You only work on what you can make a real difference to; the rest is in the lap of the gods.

Once you've completed the two circles, keep them near your desk every day so you can be reminded to focus only on those things you can actually have an impact on.

Clean and Simplify Your Environment

This is one of my favorite stress relievers. Whenever I feel overloaded mentally, I clean up my desk area, my car, and my home. I throw out whatever I can, and put the rest in neat piles or in storage. I make sure my desk area is clear and clean. Any spare clothes lying around go into the laundry bag and I do a two-minute clean-up of the bathroom and kitchen.

What a difference this quick clean makes to my mind. I definitely feel more relaxed and in charge. I have found that when I am on top of my environment I feel much more confident that I am getting on top of my life.

Furthermore, several times a year I try to reduce my possessions. I get rid of 10 percent of my clothes, twenty or so books, any extra pairs of shoes, and all but the most necessary garage boxes. I have found that generally the less I own, the more organized I feel. By doing this life simplification exercise three or four times a year rather than once every five years, I find it's easy and quick—half an hour will often do it.

So why not try this system right now. If you're reading this at work or at home, take 10 minutes right now and throw out everything you can see that you don't need. Put excess clothes into garbage bags to drop off at your local charity and throw the rest of your surplus stuff into other garbage bags.

Go!

If you do it I'm certain you'll agree with me that throwing stuff out and simplifying your immediate environment make you feel considerably more relaxed and optimistic.

Get Out in the Sunshine

Mounting evidence shows that there's a strong connection between the amount of sunlight you get and your mood. I'm not talking about getting a tan, but I am suggesting you enjoy around 20 minutes of sunlight on your face each and every day.

Cities with less sunlight, like Seattle and Stockholm, report higher levels of depression among their citizens. Countless studies have shown that when people don't receive light from the sun they feel more pessimistic. The sun affects your hormone levels, the health of your pineal gland, and your body's circadian rhythms. Time in the sun isn't a luxury—it's a necessity for a human's healthy functioning.

Even indoors, the amount of light around you has been found to affect your mood. Keep your lights bright and you'll tend to feel better. If you're really serious about boosting your mood, check out full-spectrum lighting, available from numerous websites. Full-spectrum lightbulbs closely mimic the sun's rays and therefore keep you more awake and upbeat.

Regulate Your Life

As I mentioned in Chapter Five, if your life feels out of control try regulating more parts of it. Both our body and our mind like order; in fact, our whole universe behaves generally in a beautifully ordered way. The more you do the same, the more you will be in harmony with life. (For information on this concept, investigate the ancient Chinese philosophy of Taoism.)

Try getting up at the same time each day and going to sleep at the same time each night. Keep things tidy at home. Organize your closet and bookshelf, your e-mails and your weekly calendar. You will find that as your life becomes more ordered your inner agitation will decrease and you'll begin to feel much calmer and more contented.

Some creative people love to see themselves as anarchists and rebel against the very thought of living an ordered life. If you put yourself in that category I ask you to just try the alternative for a week. I'm confident that you'll discover that you actually become much more creative when you're in a settled environment—and that your general happiness improves as well.

Eat Five Meals a Day

What you eat dramatically affects how you feel. If you eat low-nutrient foods you will have less energy, which can lead to more negative moods. It often amazes me that people who view themselves as being totally dedicated to success will cut corners in their diet. It's as if they see no connection between the fuel inside them and the performance they produce. Be clear: there is a strong correlation.

It's not just what you eat that matters, it's the time you eat, too, and how much. The fact is, if you eat five small meals a day rather than the customary three larger meals, you will find you feel considerably less stressed.

How come? It's all connected with your body's insulin levels, and digestion. Big meals often make your insulin levels spike up, which makes you tired about an hour later. Large servings of food are also tough for your body to digest and most people don't realize that digestion is one of the biggest users of energy for the body (in fact, having sex is the only activity that uses more energy).

So eat smaller meals more often and you'll find your insulin levels remain more stable, and therefore so does your mood. You'll also find you're not nearly as tired.

By the way, there's another major benefit to eating five small meals a day. You'll get a lot slimmer. I know that most people think you would actually put on weight, not lose it, eating five meals, but there's a mountain of evidence that shows that eating more often is one of the best ways of all to slim down.

This benefit has to do with our body's ancient survival mechanism, built into every human. When you're eating some food every few hours your brain believes there's no need to store as much fat for any future food shortage (this probably comes from our body's genetic memory of caveman times, when food was often hard to come by).

When you have five or six hours between meals your body believes it must store up fat in case your next meal doesn't get consumed for another day or so. So your metabolism will slow and you'll keep more weight on you. (For more information on the five-meals-a-day strategy, I recommend you read *Body for Life* by Bill Phillips, one of America's most knowledgeable fitness gurus.)

But even if you're as slim as a supermodel, you'll find eating five meals a day will make you feel happier, more energized, and definitely less stressed.

LOWER YOUR STRESS TODAY

So have a look back at the eight stress-busters in this chapter and pick three you can introduce into your life, starting today. I think you'll be pleasantly surprised at how quickly these techniques will lower your stress levels and make you feel calmer and more in control. If you have anyone close to you who's a little tense at the moment, you may want to recommend some of these concepts to them as well. And if you'd like some extra stress-busting techniques, visit www.whypeoplefail.org.

Stress and failure to achieve go hand in hand. If you take daily action to keep your stress levels under control, you are far more likely to have both the energy and the motivation to keep striving for victory.

Using the stress-reduction techniques in this chapter will definitely help keep you happy, healthy, and raring to tackle your next challenge.

few relationships

There is an area that many people who crave success, wealth, and achievement rarely think about: the power of relationships.

Many talented people think they can climb the mountain of their dreams by themselves. And at first, it seems like they are right. After all, some people *are* smarter, more energetic, and more talented than the people around them—and so they fall into the classic trap of assuming that because they seem a level above others, they don't need other people to get ahead.

The evidence, however, is the total opposite. Read any interview with a high-level entrepreneur, athlete, scientist, or artist and you'll see that they have assembled a top-notch team around them, and it is held together by strong interpersonal relationships. This group of wise advisers helps the successful person in two fundamental ways—as a knowledge base and as an emotional support system.

10 BRAINS ARE BETTER THAN ONE

Peak performers expand their own knowledge base by bringing others into their world—as counselors, idea generators, or critics of their concepts.

Top businesspeople have boards to bounce their ideas off, keep them rooted in reality, and offer them the wisdom of battle-scarred experience. Even apparently "solo" artists usually have a close cadre of people whose opinions they respect and admire, to act as a collective sounding board.

The simple truth is that if you aspire to excellence but don't have strong relationships with a team of knowledgeable advisers, you're dramatically impeding your speed of ascent to the top.

EVERYONE NEEDS FRIENDS

But it's not just for professional help that you need quality relationships—it's also for emotional sustenance.

Getting to the top has never been easy, and anyone who tells you it was is just plain lying. Success always, always takes an emotional toll. To rise faster than the rest you must inevitably encounter more obstacles than the rest—and after a few years those struggles begin to weaken you emotionally.

But when you have a group of warm, wise, and caring friends around you—relationships that have stood the tests of time and hardship—it soothes those bumps in the road enormously. At times we all need a shoulder to cry on, an ear to listen, a heart to support us. Those who try to make it solely on their own may move a little faster when things are easy, but they can find life an often overwhelming burden when the going gets tough.

Even if you do manage to get to the top, it's a pretty lonely place to be if you don't have people to share the joys of victory with. Which brings us to the nonbusiness reasons for developing quality relationships.

HUMANS AREN'T ISLANDS

All the research shows that humans are generally happier when they are around other humans. Sure, we all like our space, and some people are more independent than others, but as a rule when you have others around, you are happier. (In fact, interestingly, research shows that even those who say they prefer to be alone record higher levels of life satisfaction when they are in the company of other people.)

So forgetting career success and purely focusing on life success, one of the very best strategies you can adopt to improve the quality of your life is to increase (and deepen) your personal relationships.

Think back on your life so far. Is it not true that most of the good times you have had involved interactions with other people? In my experience, over 90 percent of the time this is the case. Humans need other humans; we are gregarious creatures. Astute people take the time to develop rich and lasting relationships with people they respect and care about and who feel the same way about them.

If we agree that both professionally and personally our success relies on quality human relationships, the next issue is how we can develop these to a high degree. First, I think it makes sense to separate your potential relationships into an inner circle and an outer circle.

THE INNER CIRCLE

Your inner circle is that group of ten or so personal and professional contacts you really value. These are the people who professionally can most help you and who personally give you the most joy, just from being around you.

Take a moment now to make two quick lists of your inner circle: list 10 people in your *professional* inner circle and 10 people in your *personal* inner circle.

Remember: these are just starting lists, so don't worry if you have trouble choosing who is on them or if you can't complete them entirely. In time, as you get used to seeing your relationships in these terms, the lists will fill themselves naturally.

Now, once you've got your two lists, it's time to focus on deepening your relationships with the people on them. The overarching number-one rule here is that frequency counts. That is, if all you do is be in contact with this Top 10 group regularly, your relationships with them will get better and better (assuming, of course, you're not stalking them!). Keep your Top 10 lists on your desk and ensure you make good contact with at least one person on them every day.

What constitutes "good" contact? Well, there's a whole host of ways you can stay in touch.

For your personal Top 10 you could invite them for a coffee or brunch, send them a "What's been happening?" e-mail or just phone to say hello.

For your professional Top 10 it's a little more complex. Good contact techniques include sending them relevant articles or books, letting them know some news about your company or industry, or e-mailing them about competitor activity. One of the best methods of keeping a relationship strong is to follow up with an e-mail or call about an aspect of their business they've told you about before. You'll surprise them with your interest, and there are few things entrepreneurs like to talk about more than their own company.

Whichever way you connect, make sure you give and don't take. Everything you do, write, or say should be oriented toward serving the other person, helping them or enabling them in some way to make their life or business better.

Where you can get it wrong is when your main aim in staying in contact with a person is just to get something out of them. Smart folks can spot this a mile off and won't want to have anything to do with someone who is just trying to sell them a product or service. But focus on helping them and you'll get plenty back, in time. As the saying goes, "The heart that gives, gathers."

Try setting aside a time each day when you work on your inner-circle relationships. It doesn't have to be an hour—usually 10 or 15 minutes daily is enough, and it really adds up over time. When you take action consistently, though, you'll be impressed at how swiftly these relationships improve.

THE OUTER CIRCLE

When it comes to your outer-circle relationships, the strategy is a little different.

Your personal outer circle is those friends and acquaintances whose company you enjoy but who are not that close to you. With this group you may spend only 10 minutes a week staying in contact, either with an e-mail or a phone call or by sending them something thoughtful. It doesn't really matter what you write or do—the main point is just to stay in touch. That way, when you are organizing a dinner or an event and you invite them, you will have enough connection with them that your time together will be easy, fun, and warm.

Your professional outer circle is much the same. These people are your work contacts—people you may need to call upon occasionally for help, advice, or favors. Send them little hellos, occasional cards or quotes you find of interest. Just make sure you're contacting the people on this list about once a month so that they build up a reservoir of goodwill toward you in their mind. Once you get used to contacting them monthly, it becomes quite effortless to do so and results in a significant increase in the reach and power of your professional network. With a series of small actions, you will end up getting a vast return over time.

Regularly staying in touch with your inner and outer circles will have a mighty impact on your life. Your happiness will increase markedly as your personal relationships get richer through consistent contact. And your career rise will become much easier when you have well-oiled relationships with a large and influential base of executives and industry experts.

EXPANDING CIRCLES

The next area worth looking at is your personal and professional "expanding circles." These are two smaller circles in which you put a handful of people you don't yet have a strong relationship with (perhaps you haven't even met them) but would like to.

Constantly expanding all your circles is healthy for both your personal life and your career. It does, however, take considerable work to build relationships from scratch, so I suggest starting with just two or three people in the personal and professional circles.

With these people, less is often more. Throw out an occasional invitation or e-mail to them and then wait to see if they respond with enthusiasm. Never push too hard when opening a new relationship. If you can add a handful of new, quality people to your inner or outer circles each year, you are doing well.

WORK ON YOUR WORK COLLEAGUES

What about the men and women at work? How do you build better relationships with them? After all, it can't just be a matter of improving the amount of contact—the contact is almost constant already.

Well, there are many strategies worth trying, but let me put forward three that I have found to be highly effective.

1. *Appreciate them.* This is so simple, but so effective. Train yourself to notice when your coworkers do something well, and take a moment to warmly acknowledge them for it. People crave appreciation but rarely receive it in today's fast-paced workplace. It may only be a line or two from you, but some people will fondly remember you for it for years. (By the way, showing genuine appreciation to people with whom you have had a checkered relationship in the past can often substantially improve how you get along with each other. It's hard to dislike someone who seems to like and value you.)

   Even better, acknowledge them in front of other people—it will often make them glow with pride. When I did army training at school one of the best leadership strategies they taught was, "Praise in public, criticize in private." Over the years I've seen many managers do the opposite, with devastating results on team morale.

2. *Really listen.* One of the greatest compliments you can give someone is to listen—really listen—to what they are saying. In this world of e-mails, BlackBerries, and constant distraction, getting people's full attention is a rarity. But when you fully focus on one person, and they see that you are totally committed to hearing what they have to say, it makes them feel really special and valued. In return, they will respect and warm to you much more. One of the reasons often cited for why Bill Clinton was such a charismatic leader is that when people met him they felt as if they had his full, undivided attention, and that for that moment he really cared about what they were saying. Deep listening is a powerful technique.

3. *Be upbeat.* Humans are very sensitive to energy. When someone at work is always down emotionally, we usually don't want to be around them even if they are really good at their job. Correspondingly, we love to hang around positive, fun, upbeat people. They give us energy, lift our moods, make tough projects seem attainable, and make challenging workplaces more bearable.

    Being upbeat is one of the easiest and quickest ways to make a positive impact on your relationships in the office (and with your company's clients). Yet it's also one of the least-practiced relationship-building methods. Now I'm certainly not suggesting you leap around the office screaming like a football coach or laughing like a circus clown—merely that you act empowered and dynamic, seek the good in tough situations, endeavor to lift others up a little emotionally, and expect the best from both people and situations.

    Truly, if you just focus on behaving in an upbeat way for one month you will find that the quality of your professional relationships (and indeed of your personal ones) will be transformed. In life, it is not always the smartest or hardest-working person who gets to the top—it is often the most positive and likable who makes it to the highest levels.

By verbally appreciating the people you work with, sincerely and attentively listening to them, and being upbeat emotionally around them you will soon find that your influence and impact at work increase significantly.

LITTLE THINGS, BIG RESULTS

It's important to remember that none of these techniques requires huge amounts of effort. Just a minute here, a minute there focusing on any of these tactics can yield substantial dividends. Here are a few more methods that can massively improve the caliber of your relationships.

Compliment People to Others

When you say good things about a person to others, it soon gets back to that person and makes them feel terrific inside. There are few things we like more than hearing that someone else thinks highly of us. Let me stress that I'm not suggesting you just make up compliments about a person and voice them to everyone who knows that person—that would be pathetically insincere. I'm recommending that if you genuinely feel positively about a person, make sure you let the people around them know.

Smile Often

We humans are innately programmed to feel more safe and comfortable around people who smile at us. It's part of our brain's way of recognizing a friend. When you smile, you also encourage people to think you are both confident and competent. A warm smile can disarm many a tense business negotiation or personal altercation. It brings any stressful scenario down a notch or two. In a society where so many people are close to their mental breaking point, a simple smile can be a powerful antidote to the everyday intensity of life.

Touch People Occasionally

There's loads of research that shows people respond more favorably when they are lightly touched (for example, I once read a study that showed that waiters who briefly touch their restaurant patrons receive bigger tips). Touching seems to affect us positively at a subconscious level. We are rarely aware when someone does it, but it can make us feel more warmly about that person afterwards. Don't take it too far, though. I once touched a potential client in an important business presentation and he physically recoiled in horror. Some people just don't like to be touched. However, used occasionally, especially with people with whom you interact regularly, it can be a surprisingly effective technique.

Remember the Emotional Bank Account

View your relationships like bank accounts. If you're always making withdrawals (asking for favors, seeking help, not being nice), eventually the account will run dry. But if you're always looking for ways to add to the account (by doing things for someone, giving them your time, and making them feel good), the emotional bank account will be healthy. Always search for what you can contribute to another person before looking to gain any advantage for yourself. Paradoxically, if you look after their side first you will have a much stronger chance of getting what you eventually seek—and often more than you seek.

Seek First to Understand, Then to Be Understood

This is a classic technique from the great leadership expert Stephen Covey. Many of our relationship problems stem from our desire to get our point across rather than fully appreciate the other person's point of view. Turn that attitude around and start putting yourself in other people's shoes. How do they feel? What do they hope for or expect? When you look at social interactions through this lens, the depth of the relationships you have with those around you is immediately enhanced. Smart people can sense when you're there to solve their issues and not just your own. Interacting with this attitude strengthens the bonds of trust and lays the foundation for sturdy, long-term relationships.

Become a Student of Psychology

Relationship building is like any other aspect of life: the more you study it, the stronger it gets. Fortunately, in the last twenty years there has been great progress in the study of the human psyche and how to influence it. If you want to vastly improve the quality of your relationships, I suggest you investigate fields such as cognitive behavior therapy, neurolinguistic programming, Buddhist philosophy, and sports psychology. Each of them contains a precious reservoir of wisdom that can dramatically improve all your relationships. Like anything else in life, with relationships it pays to learn from the experts. When you first delve into some of these concepts they may seem weird or even outlandish, but bear with them. The reason they have stood the test of time is because millions of people have tested them and found them to work.

A COMMITMENT TO MASTERY

In summary, if you wish to avoid failure in any area that's important to you, it's imperative that you make a real commitment to mastering the art of interpersonal relationships. You simply can't make it to the top by yourself. You must engage the assistance of a multitude of others along the way—and the quality of the people you can get to help you will largely depend on your ability to develop strong interpersonal relationships.

The exciting thing is that relationship building is an area that very few people ever seek excellence in. So if you devote serious time to gaining expertise in this arena, you will soon find that you have an array of success tools that your competition in life just can't match. These skills will be applicable in any domain of life—business, personal, or family—and usually work equally well in all of them.

Strong relationships are the glue that keeps the rest of the pieces of the success puzzle together. Master relationship building and you will be well on your way to mastering success.

lack of persistence

Surely one of the most crucial reasons people ultimately fail is that they give up too soon.

When it comes down to it, it's giving up early in the attempt that is at the heart of failure. Not that the goal couldn't be achieved. Not that it was too difficult. But simply because the person stopped trying far too early.

There are two reasons people don't persist with goals. The first is poor self-image. Deep down they don't have faith that they are capable of pulling off a great victory, so when they try, they do so in a tentative, half-hearted manner and are ready to give up at the first sign of difficulty.

This, unfortunately, is the majority of people. After ten years of lukewarm effort at various dreams, they conclude that high achievement is just too darn hard and they settle for a life of general mediocrity rather than use the pain of failure to achieve again. But if we were to take a close look at how they tried to progress, we would see that in many cases it was their persistence that was flawed, not that the goal was impossible to achieve.

I don't want to be too hard on these people, because the truth is that I applaud any effort at all to succeed. It takes guts even to begin to go for a dream. I also think our education system is largely to blame. After more than a decade of schooling, were we ever taught even one class specifically on how to succeed? Were we ever taught the awesome power of persistence? Well, I sure wasn't. That's really disgraceful because if students just mastered that one lesson—how to persist intelligently until you reach your goal—their entire lives would be improved.

The second reason people don't persist is that they believe there is something wrong with failure.

AVOIDING FAILURE

The typical person's view of failure is that it shouldn't happen. They believe that if they fail at something then that is terrible. So it's no surprise that after they fail three or four times their emotions get low and they're ready to give up.

But contrast that attitude to the mindset of a high achiever. When champions go for a goal, before they even start out they know they are going to fail numerous times. They comprehend that all substantial success is built on the back of failure. This is absolutely clear in their mind, so when they encounter an obstacle they are not surprised or concerned. They expect bad things to happen—lots of bad things—and know they must create solutions to these roadblocks, not just give up and stop.

In part, our culture and media are to blame. Our society publicizes and praises the winners in life and rarely looks at how many times these people lost on their way to the winner's podium. The countless failures of most businesspeople, athletes, scientists, investors, and artists are almost never talked about. Instead, we see magazine articles and TV programs about how special these superstars are, how talented. (Indeed, plenty of times these kinds of simplistic, inaccurate portraits are encouraged by the winners themselves.)

What is the result of all this worshipping of the successful? The rest of us think that those people are better than we are. After all, here we are struggling in the trenches, fighting to make any progress at all, while we read and watch stories about people who appear to be achieving their goals effortlessly.

Well, don't you believe it. I have never, ever met a person who's had lasting success who didn't encounter failure, hardship, and disappointment frequently along the way. They may not talk about it—they may even try to hide it—but it is there nevertheless.

The ever-present dark shadow of failure needs to be brought into the open. Our society needs to be taught not to fear failure but to embrace it as a natural occurrence on the road to every success. If everyone understood that failure is a normal and customary part of high achievement, they wouldn't give up so quickly. They would certainly be more likely to persist.

Pause for a moment and ask yourself these important questions.

What is my attitude to failure? Do I avoid it? Am I scared of it?
How is my attitude towards failure affecting my current actions, goals, and rate of success? Am I truly persistent?

In my own life I have had many failures. I've been sacked. I've been close to broke. I've been ridiculed by my peers in my industry. I've been totally out of my depth. I've not reached literally hundreds of goals. As a result, I've had two choices: either give up and settle for average results, or learn how to persist and eventually achieve at a high level. I chose the second option, although it's not been an easy road to travel.

A TWO-STAGE PROCESS

What I would like to show you now is a two-stage process for learning how to become a master of persistence. This is exciting, because when you think about it, if you were to become such a master, all aspects of your life would rise to a much higher level. If you become a master of persistence you will earn more, achieve more, and enjoy more. Quantitatively and qualitatively you will experience a better life.

It isn't a complex system, but it is remarkably effective. I assure you that if you focus on my persistence system every day for a month, it will become part of your habitual thinking patterns. Once it becomes a habit, your results will go through the roof.

The first stage is purely mental—it's a way of looking at yourself.

Be Determined

Every time you look in the mirror, I want you to say to yourself, "I am UNRELENTING." See yourself as someone who never quits, never gives up. Someone who is so determined that no obstacle can stop you. Say it, think it, every time you see yourself in a mirror.

If you can just train yourself to do this, you will notice a change in your performance within days. Truly, you will begin to see yourself differently.

Decades of research have shown that we perform in line with our self-image, but that this self-image is not set in stone. You can sculpt, refine, and improve it. This simple technique applied day after day will do just that. And when your image of who you are changes, then your actions will change. Once your actions improve, inevitably so will your results.

Actually, most people are talking to themselves already when they look in the mirror, but too often they are saying negative things. Stop that! Take charge. Rebuild your self-image, starting by telling yourself that you are an absolute master of persistence. You are absolutely unrelenting.

The second stage to improving your persistence is to follow my 5-Step Persistence Model.

The Persistence Model

I believe that if you follow this process you will be much more effective in the way that you persist, and therefore you will achieve much better, faster results. Once again, it's certainly not a complex method, but I think you'll agree that it's likely to improve your level of effectiveness substantially.

If you are working on any major goal and encounter an obstacle, I advocate you do five things.

Step 1: Repeat Your Efforts

By this I mean try exactly the same thing again and again. It may astonish you, but the vast majority of people do not do this. They quit at the very first sign of resistance. Very often when a strategy fails, the strategy itself is not wrong—it's just that for one reason or another you didn't get the result you anticipated.

For example, one of my biggest career breaks was becoming the creative director of an advertising agency at age 21. That is between ten and twenty years earlier than most people achieve this goal, and only 5 percent of creatives in the industry ever reach that level.

The reality is that the company that offered me the job was not the first organization I had approached. Just a few weeks earlier, I had put forward exactly the same concept to another advertising agency, but had been rejected. By simply repeating my presentation to another company I ended up with a spectacular new job.

So you should remember that sometimes your strategy is right—it just hasn't been repeated enough.

Step 2: Change Strategies

A simple enough concept: after trying the same strategy several times, change strategy. Hey, success isn't brain surgery! But as basic as this tactic is, we are all guilty of not following it at various times in our life. We may persist, but we do the same thing again and again and again, usually getting the same abysmal outcome.

As writer Rita Mae Brown said, "Insanity is doing the same thing, over and over again, but expecting different results."

Are you guilty of this currently, in your relationship, health, or career? Most of us are guilty of it in some way or another. Once you're aware of the concept it's usually pretty easy to spot your errors and change your strategy, but the initial awareness that you're repeating the same thing over and over is the hard part.

Now, if all you did was these two steps of the process, I am certain you would get vastly better results in all areas of your life. But we have three important steps to go.

Step 3: Model the Best

It doesn't matter what you're trying to achieve—there are plenty of people throughout the history of the world who have achieved similar goals before you. So copy them. Model what the best do and you're likely to get similar results.

They could be your direct business competitors, or maybe an overseas company that's the absolute best in your field. It could even be someone outstanding in your own company. It doesn't have to be a business-related goal, either. If you have a goal of improving a personal relationship, model anyone you know who seems to have achieved that same thing. Have coffee with them, get their advice, learn to think like they think.

Remember: you really need just one new idea, one extra strategy, to totally revolutionize your results. And the best place to look for such gems of wisdom is among people who have already excelled in that area. That's why reading books written by experts in your field is so important. These people have made many of the mistakes you are destined to make in the future. If you can read their stories, take their advice, and heed their warnings, you can literally cut years off the time it takes to reach the top. Read with a pen in hand to highlight important points and write ideas you're going to try on a sheet of paper to remind you to take action. You'll be amazed at what great ideas you find when you learn from the royalty in your field.

You don't have to search the world for examples of excellence to model, either. Look among your friends, or the staff in your office. Who gets better results than you? What do they do differently? How could you copy them and get similar results? As the great human performance expert Jim Rohn likes to say, "Success leaves clues."

Most people don't think this way—they try to pioneer their own way to success. This is a brave but not intelligent way to persist. Modeling the best in any area of life enables you to improve faster and with less stress.

Step 4: Maintain Positivity

There are two ways to achieve your goal. Both work, but only one is enjoyable.

1. You can work yourself into the ground, trying everything but feeling miserable about your prospects of achievement. Eventually, because you keep on trying you often end up achieving your goal, but you don't enjoy the process.
2. Or you could assume you're going to achieve your goal, expect that things are going to go your way, and decide you are going to have fun on this journey no matter what. Then take lots of action.

Both methods are effective, but the first strategy will become very emotionally draining over time, whereas the second will be exciting and uplifting.

Choosing to be positive as you persist with a tough task is a small choice that creates a profoundly different experience. And believe me, it is just a choice. You don't have to get depressed when things are going badly—we humans always have the choice to decide our thinking, regardless of the prevailing circumstances. Please never forget that.

One of the best paradigms you can take on is that life is a game, not a war. By simply thinking about the world as a game, you'll find you will loosen up and lighten up about the hardships of life. Those who see life as a war may win many victories, but they will do so with tension and self-imposed pressure. It's a tough way to live.

Furthermore, if you choose the second way of thinking because you are expecting a victory down the road, you are far more likely to keep persisting than if you see the road forward as difficult and unlikely to be fruitful.

Step 5: Return to the Vision

This is really important. Sometimes we get so immersed in doing tasks that we lose track of the big picture—the very reason we're working so hard to achieve stuff in the first place. Then, because we have stopped thinking about a grand future for our life, we get overwhelmed by the countless obstacles and hardships we are facing.

When this happens to you (and let's face it—it happens to all of us at some point), it's vital that you return to your higher vision. Truly, one of the best ways you can lift any mild depression you may have is by focusing your mind on where you hope to be in three years. By regularly immersing yourself in inspiring and uplifting thoughts about how you want your life to be, any challenges you are facing will seem less daunting. It's a great mood lifter.

Your big vision doesn't have to be three years—it could be one year, or ten. It could even be your vision of how you'd like your life to turn out as you come to the end of your journey on the planet. But three years is a good length of time for most people. It's far enough into the future that you will have time to achieve some remarkable things, yet close enough to feel that you'll get there relatively soon.

People who achieve magnificent futures don't do so by accident. They do so because they create an exciting vision for how they want their lives to be, then maintain their focus on it every day as they take the many little and often boring steps to make their dream a reality. This blending of vision with actions is crucial, and if you examine anyone who fails, you will usually see a weakness in one of these two areas.

So that is the 5-Step Persistence Model. I hope you'll see that it's a far more intelligent way to achieve your goals than the usual "try, try, try again" model. You may want to type and print out the five steps and put them next to your computer or bathroom mirror so that you look at them each day (I find little written reminders hugely helpful in keeping me focused on the things that really matter).

While we're on the subject of persistence, here are a few more powerful strategies to help you persist when things get tough.

DO A TINY BIT OF YOUR TASK

Sometimes all we need is a bit of momentum. If you've not done any work on a project because you just can't stand the thought of it, resolve to do just one single part of it, no matter how small.

Maybe it's making just one call. Perhaps it's merely creating a to-do list for the project. Possibly it's just gathering all the tools and information you need to start. By taking even one tiny step towards your goal, you'll feel a sense of progress. And plenty of times that momentum will encourage you to take more steps.

Sometimes if I'm unmotivated I'll spend just 10 minutes on five tasks in a row, two minutes on each. I'll do a quick clean-up, arrange a meeting, brainstorm some fun things to do on the weekend, and quickly jot down my goals for the year. It's really amazing how many projects you can move forward in just 10 minutes if you're creative and dynamic about it. These little steps often make you feel fantastic inside because you get a real sense of achievement from making progress in so many areas in such a short period of time.

GET ASSISTANCE

We all want to achieve our goals on our own. But "we" is almost always stronger than "me." It's usually far more effective for several people to work on a problem, swapping ideas, solutions, and points of view. So if you're having trouble persisting, call in the cavalry. Phone a friend you respect and ask for his or her advice. E-mail acknowledged experts in the field and seek their opinion (you'll be amazed how many superstars in the field will take the time to help you out).

Maybe even create your own mastermind group that meets weekly or monthly to solve each other's challenges and offer encouraging words to other members of the group. Many of history's greatest solo achievers actually had a whole team of trusted advisers helping them behind the scenes.

Life is so much harder when you try to do it all alone. You should know also that people who don't often hang around others are usually less happy and less healthy than folks who have a strong support group around them. Humans in general are gregarious—we're designed to work together, not alone. If you're having trouble persisting, maybe you need to bring in some supporters and cheerleaders.

FOCUS ON WHAT REALLY MATTERS

Of all the tasks you're working on, only a few of them really count. Sometimes when you're feeling totally overwhelmed by a project it's easy to forget that. Instead you get caught in a quagmire of hundreds of tasks that in the end really aren't going to make much difference to your final results. Perhaps it's time to do much less, but do a few things really well.

Is the most important ingredient to your business success making new calls? Then forget most of your other tasks, and just do twice as much new client calling.

What is the one thing that would improve your relationship the most? Spend less time on the other stuff and really focus on that.

The key here is clarity. When you ask someone the number one most important aspect of their job—health, success, relationship, spiritual life, or family life—they usually have never even thought about it. But if you meet somebody who is totally clear on his or her number one priority in each area of life, it's pretty likely that this person is more effective, more successful, and happier than most. Such clarity leads to greater efficiency, which leads to greater progress in areas they care about, which naturally leads to greater life satisfaction.

Are you focusing on what really counts?

REST

If you're having difficulty persisting, it's no sin to take a break. That could mean just making sure you take 30 minutes for lunch every workday, or it could mean giving yourself a few weeks away from your project and working on something else for a while.

Many people cannot bring themselves to do this. Their work ethic won't allow them to take it easy. It's in their self-image that they must struggle, struggle, struggle onward, no matter the pain.

That's kind of noble, but it's also silly. All kinds of research indicate that humans perform better after a decent rest. That's just how we're made. If you fail to rest properly your enthusiasm will eventually sag and your performance will diminish. Soon after, your willpower to persist will decline considerably too.

Take plenty of breaks, big and small. The truth is, your subconscious mind will be working on your problems even while you take a break from them; it will be processing data and reorganizing to help you upon your return. Resting effectively is crucial to ongoing persistence.

DON'T FORGET TO EXERCISE

It may seem strange to suggest that exercising affects your persistence, but I strongly believe it does. There's a huge correlation between how negatively you see aspects of your life and how fit you are. When you're tired it's easy to not persist. As General George S. Patton put it, "Fatigue makes cowards of us all."

Don't make this mistake. Put your health first in your life and ironically you'll end up achieving more than if you had put achievement first.

I find that when I'm working out most days, my attitude towards my tasks and goals is much more positive and proactive. I am simply more motivated to achieve when I feel vibrantly healthy. If you're feeling like your goals are virtually hopeless, go for a run, take a yoga class, hit the weights—anything to get your body moving. You'll come back to your task with more energy and more willpower to get the job done.

I'm not saying you have to spend five hours a week working out (although I'd recommend it). Any exercise is better than nothing. Even 10 minutes a day is going to make a gigantic difference to your levels of optimism and urge to persist. Exercise really is that transformative.

REWARD YOURSELF

The problem with shooting for a big goal is that it often takes months, if not years, to reach it. In the meantime all you can see ahead of you are endless obstacles and mountainous challenges. It can be disheartening for even the most ambitious among us.

If you start on a goal with great relish but then find after a while that you run out of steam and lose your drive, there's a powerful technique to help you keep moving towards your aim: create a system of rewards at each step along the way.

These rewards could be daily, like promising yourself you'll watch a movie if you can get three major tasks finished by 5 PM, or treating yourself to a delicious pastry if you can make 10 new business cold calls. Or your rewards could be monthly, like giving yourself a weekend away as a pat on the back for four weeks of solid work.

By planning a system of little and big rewards you'll often find your short-term motivation increases considerably. It makes working hard more fun and enjoyable, more like a game than a struggle. The trick with this system is not to give in and allow yourself the reward even if you don't hit your target. Be strict with yourself and the reward will have real power to motivate you to keep going just a little longer.

Take a minute or two and write down 10 nice rewards you could give yourself as you reach different stages of your goal.

Even just writing them down will probably make you feel a little excited, as you think of experiencing all these cool things. Success doesn't have to be a struggle—it really can be fun if you create fun moments along the way. One of the very best ways to do this is with a tempting rewards system.

If any of these strategies appeal to you, grab them and start making them a part of your life immediately.

IT'S NOT LUCK

I'm sure you're beginning to see that success really isn't down to chance. By applying proven ideas and systems to your life, you can dramatically increase the likelihood of achieving your dreams. We can take control of our future and change our results simply by putting a handful of techniques into action and applying them daily in our lives. Failures don't do this. Failures have no systems for managing their mind, body, or actions. They are reactive, not proactive. They are haphazard, not systematic. Sporadic, not consistent.

Don't fall into this trap. Memorize these persistence-increasing techniques and really try to make them core elements of your life. If you slip up, that's fine—we all do, often. Just pick yourself up and get back on track fast.

Resolve deep in your heart that you will become a master of persistence. Commit to being unrelenting in your actions, totally unstoppable. Then you will one day come to a point when you look around and realize that you have not just achieved your dreams, but have gone further than you ever dared to imagine.

money obsession

I have a question for you: why exactly did you buy this book?

Was it to help you become richer? There's nothing at all wrong with that. Who doesn't want to experience more of life's nice material pleasures? But at the same time we all need to be careful about becoming slaves to money.

Growing evidence shows that the urge for wealth is reaching extreme levels in our society and is in fact taking over the lives of many people. The net result of this craving for cash is that literally millions of people are living lives that are anything but successful. They are instead becoming true failures—unhappy, stressed, and feeling ever more alone.

Never before in modern history have so many been so obsessed with getting wealthier. We want better cars, bigger houses, more toys, more experiences, more jewelry, fancier clothes . . . the list is endless and ever increasing. These desires are often fuelled by television shows profiling the rich, magazines pushing luxury lifestyles, and of course endless advertisements promising a better life if we just purchase this or that product.

This avalanche of "desire media" has collectively hypnotized half the planet, so that many of us get up in the morning with one primary aim: to get richer. This would be fine if seeking riches led to happiness, but the truth is in fact exactly the opposite. Decades of research clearly show that focusing on acquiring material goods is making us more unhappy than ever. We are being sold a totally false fairy tale, a gingerbread house with a thousand witches hiding inside.

THE FACTS ABOUT MONEY

Sure, we should all strive to improve our lives (I think you'll agree that the vast majority of this book is focused on that very aim), but if we focus entirely on money and what it buys, we will have made a mistake of catastrophic proportions.

Let's take a look at the cold, hard realities behind the modern world's obsession with wealth by examining what independent scientific research has concluded on the subject. Thankfully there is now a huge body of data on the impact of materialism on happiness. In the next few pages I'll take you through the most interesting and relevant studies. Fasten your seatbelts—you're going to be shocked at what you read.

Fact: Money Doesn't Increase Happiness

We've heard this said since we were kids, but how many of us actually believe it? Not many, judging by how most of us live our lives. As Oscar Wilde said, "There is only one class in the community that thinks more about money than the rich, and that is the poor. The poor can think of nothing else."

Truth be told, we're all thinking about money much of the day—how to make it, how to save it, and how to avoid losing it. That's understandable. Many people are under pressure just to pay their bills, so a certain level of focus on money is absolutely necessary for our survival. But focusing our entire lives on financial accumulation is a huge mistake, as the following research study shows.

Professors Tim Kasser and Richard Ryan interviewed groups of people from a variety of economic backgrounds who were living in Rochester, New York. They found that those who focused on money, image, and fame reported less vitality and more depression than those who were not as concerned with those values. So these people thought focusing on money and fame would make them happier, but the reverse proved to be true. As Kasser noted, "The more materialistic values are at the centre of our lives, the more our quality of life is diminished."

It's not just an American phenomenon. Studies conducted in Germany, India, Britain, Denmark, South Korea, and Russia all indicate the same thing—that materialistic values and well-being rarely go together.

In Australia, it's the same. Researchers Shaun Saunders and Don Munro carried out a series of studies with Aussie students. Yet again, they discovered that when students had a materialistic outlook they had greater feelings of anxiety, depression, and even anger than other students.

And in the mother of all student happiness studies, renowned well-being researchers Ed Diener and Shige Oishi collected data from students from 41 different countries. The result? More damning evidence that people who focused on material stuff were less satisfied with their lives.

One of the most intriguing studies on happiness and materialism occurred when researchers looked at the connection between the introduction of television and well-being. The states that got TV early developed dramatically higher crime rates than states which had TV introduced in later years. When researchers examined the statistics they found that in every case when TV was introduced, the next year crime rates went up in that state.

Why? Well, I believe it's because thanks to their new TVs people saw many goods that they'd never thought about owning before, as well as people enjoying luxurious lifestyles they could only dream about living—and as they became more materialistically minded, some turned to crime to get the products and lifestyles they craved.

Professor Kasser and his colleagues believe that materialism is a coping strategy. When people feel insecure or anxious they pursue materialistic stuff, believing it will help reduce the negativity they feel. (Perhaps you also feel this, deep down inside.) The problem is that mounting evidence concludes that looking to make more money will not reduce these feelings at all—it will usually make them worse.

Fact: We Are Rarely Satisfied with the Money We Have

You might be thinking, "I can see how that may be the case for most people, but not for me. I know that if I just had $10 million, that would be enough. I could stop, relax, and just enjoy what I'd made for the rest of my life."

Nice in theory, but not backed up by the statistics. The research indicates that no matter how large the amount we have earned, we will only be satisfied with it for a short period of time. Pretty soon we'll start dreaming of earning even more. Our desire for wealth often becomes insatiable. How else can we explain the multibillionaires who still yearn to make even more and rise even higher on the Forbes 400 list of the world's richest?

(Incidentally, in case you thought those super-rich were happier than you or me, think again. They most definitely are not. Diener researched 49 of the mega-wealthy on the Forbes rich list and found that they were on average merely 1 percent happier than the average American wage earner!)

There's a famous study by Philip Brickman on lottery winners. He compared the happiness of those who'd won the lottery with others who lived nearby. His conclusion? The winners were no happier than average people in their neighborhood. Actually, many of the lottery winners proved to be *less* happy with their everyday lives.

Arie Kapteyn and Tom Wansbeck also conducted some excellent research on how much money people would be satisfied with. They asked people from a variety of income levels how much money they required to meet their needs. The conclusion was that wealthier people believed they needed more than poorer people. In other words, they had become used to a certain level of living—it was their new norm.

It seems we soon adjust to whatever level of wealth we have risen to. Once it becomes normal to be at that level, we seek higher and higher levels of wealth to satisfy us. It becomes a vicious (and expensive) cycle.

Is our addiction to increasing our wealth any different from a drunk's addiction to wine? Maybe not. Some people certainly crave money like an alcoholic craves booze. The only difference is that the thirst for ever-increasing wealth is condoned, even applauded, by society, whereas the alcoholic's addiction is frowned upon. Sure, the typical person's addiction to making cash may not be nearly as intense as an alcoholic's addiction, but it is there nevertheless.

Ask yourself this question: could you stop trying to get wealthier even if you wanted to? Really? If you even paused before you gave your answer, you are in danger of living a life of low happiness, as the research so damningly shows.

Fact: High Materialism Can Affect Your Health

You won't just be less happy, you may be more sickly, too. Once again, there is a serious amount of research backing up this notion. Simply summarized, materialistic people tend to have worse health than non-materialistic people. What kinds of health problems do materialistic people experience?

Less energy and vitality. The research shows that many materialistic people have less get-up-and-go and enthusiasm for life than the average person.

More depression. Hardly surprising. It's tough to keep striving and striving to obtain more and more prizes and gold. After a while it gets you down.

Higher cholesterol and greater risk of heart disease. After twenty years of going for the cash, it's no wonder the heart starts to get overloaded by the stress.

Greater use of tobacco, drugs, and alcohol. Hey, you have to get relief from your pain somehow. Many people look to artificial mood-changing substances to pep them up a bit.

Just one of these health problems would be tough to handle, but plenty of people have all of these symptoms at once! Not a pleasant experience, but a common one among those who build their lives around acquiring much more than other people. The truth is, being deeply materialistic is physically and mentally exhausting. These people spend all day trying to get more, sleep a little at night, then do it all over again, day after day, year after year, decade after decade.

Here's a curious thing: many people who experience a heart attack say it was the best thing that happened to them. Many say that only something life-threatening like a heart attack could have woken them up to the materialistic, selfish, exhausting life they were leading and motivated them to get off the money treadmill.

Don't wait for such a wake-up call to happen to you. Evaluate your lifestyle seriously right now. Is striving for wealth costing you your health? There's an old saying: "People ruin their health to get wealth, but then would give up all of their wealth to regain their health." Sad, but so true.

It doesn't have to be an either/or situation, of course. Plenty of people achieve enormous wealth and are both mentally and physically in tip-top condition. It can certainly be done. But if you feel that your health is slipping as you pursue riches every day, today is the day you should reevaluate your goals. Believe me: if you get sick, all the money in the world will appear worthless in comparison to your health. You know it, so live it.

We've established that putting money first usually makes you less happy, less satisfied, and less healthy. So what drives someone to focus on getting rich in the first place? Well, by now it won't come as a shock to discover that there's been loads of intriguing research done on this aspect of materialism. And the results aren't pretty.

FILLING A VOID

In general, if someone seeks great wealth and fame it's because of neediness—a strong feeling that somehow they're not good enough as they are and they therefore need to own more, to be more, both in their own mind and in the perception of those around them.

Some of these feelings are a result of upbringing. For example, it's been shown that teenagers who are materialistic usually had parents who weren't particularly nurturing. Their parents didn't acknowledge them as much, didn't give them many choices. They also often had parents who were overly possessive and gave them little structure in their lives. As a result, these children were more likely to feel insecure.

Interestingly, it's not coming from a wealthy family that makes people materialistic—in fact, quite the opposite. Coming from an environment of poverty is much more likely to lead to obsessive materialism.

NOT LOVING YOURSELF

Another reason a person might feel they must get rich at almost any cost is because they have feelings of low self-worth.

How does low self-esteem develop in humans? Well, the data is clear on this. If you grow up in an environment with little emotional warmth or with unloving parents, you're far more likely to suffer from self-esteem problems. If you feel neglected as a child, then low self-esteem can easily arise in later life.

So what often happens is that a person with low self-esteem attempts to lift it by achieving something remarkable (like becoming rich or famous). When that occurs they feel better about themselves—at least for a while. But once they've linked nicer feelings about themselves with material achievements, if they're not careful they get hooked on that feeling and end up seeking similar experiences for the rest of their lives.

The net result? A life of endless striving and neediness, usually ending in mental exhaustion.

DEPENDENT ON OTHERS

Such people often have what is known in behavioral science circles as
"contingent self-esteem." In plain language, this means their self-esteem
depends on what others think of them. These people believe that if they
could only get wealthy or famous then others would love them, or at
least respect them. And so they dedicate years of their lives to grasping
for such riches, with predictably depressing results. Once they reach a
certain level of wealth, they find it isn't making them any happier. So
they try to make even more money. Inevitably they still don't feel
great about themselves and so their dissatisfaction can end up lower
than ever.

Then there's those who suffer from the "social comparison" problem.
Some people achieve great wealth and then start hanging out with the
ultra-rich. As they look around at their new friends they realize they
themselves may be wealthy, but the people around them are far wealthier again. In comparison they're not outstandingly rich at all. So what
do they do? They start clamoring for even more money, fame, or pres-
tige, just to keep up with their new peers.

That's why you'll often meet people worth, say, $50 million who
actually don't think they have enough money—because compared to
their pals down at the yacht club they are actually poor.

There is enormous potential for this wealth chase to be an endless
cycle. In fact, it's almost guaranteed, particularly if nobody ever points
out the stupidity of behaving like this. It often amazes me that so many
highly intelligent people have put themselves on this never-ending
treadmill of suffering, completely unaware that the real reason they're
doing it is their low self-worth.

If they actually took the time to work on themselves, look deep
inside and see that they are being driven by self-esteem issues, then they
could act to fix them. But most people don't. They are too busy trying
to make more moolah to even stop and ask themselves why they are
spending their lives in this way. They are unconscious puppets to their
inner drives. It's an ugly picture.

But enough of the bad stuff. If the search for money and fame doesn't make us happy, what does?

HAPPINESS BOOSTERS

I have studied the science of happiness for quite a few years and the reality is there are many things that are not connected with wealth that can increase our happiness. Let me give you six of the biggest happiness boosters.

Happiness Booster 1: Connect with People

Humans are meant to be with other humans. We're social creatures. Sure, there are times when we want to be alone and enjoy a little peace and quiet, but usually we like to be around others. The research shows that when people take the time to nurture three or four close, meaningful relationships they will usually be happier than those who are loners.

It's easy to see why. If you cultivate a few deep friendships, when things get rough in life you have someone to console and support you. When you experience a wonderful event, you have someone to share your joy with. And in between the ups and downs of life you have someone just to have a laugh with.

Be clear on this. If you want to quickly improve your happiness, then start spending more time with others. If you need to develop some more friendships, then do two simple things: be interested in other people, and be upbeat. Just focusing on these two aspects will make most people delighted to be your pal. Try it. You'll be amazed how well it works.

Happiness Booster 2: Practice Gratitude

Every morning and evening, take a few minutes to think about all the good things that are happening in your world. It's almost impossible to feel depressed when you're being grateful. Give it a go—you'll see it's true. By constantly focusing on how good life is and being thankful for it, your dark moods will lift fast.

Now you may think your life is so hard right now that you have absolutely zero to be thankful for. What a load of rubbish! Be thankful for your eyes. Be thankful you live in a free country. Be thankful you can afford to eat (millions can't). When you put your mind to it, there are literally thousands of good things our Creator has given us that we can be thankful for—if only we take the time to appreciate them.

Happiness Booster 3: Help Other People

Renowned psychologist Dr. Martin Seligman has some great research on this. He got his students to do one charitable act and one act that only benefited themselves. He then asked them to report back on which one made them feel happier. Interestingly, every one of his students reported that performing the charitable act made them feel vastly better than performing the selfish act.

But don't just do the occasional nice thing for others. Make it more regular by joining a community group, agreeing to meet friends weekly to help them, or setting a goal to help 10 people a month. You'll find the more nice things you do for others, the happier you feel. (This is not just me trying to be saintly—it's backed up by many different behavioral studies.)

Why does doing good make you feel good? Well, one of the best answers to that question was written by psychologist Victor Frankl in his masterpiece, *Man's Search for Meaning*. Frankl showed that people want to live with a real sense of purpose—they want a vision to live by. And when that vision is centered around helping other people or the community as a whole, that makes you feel terrific. If, however, all you are living for is the next dollar or the next toy, then life quickly becomes a downer.

Happiness Booster 4: Increase Omega-3

Diet has a huge influence on how happy you feel. For instance, if you eat lots of simple sugars your body's insulin levels will rocket up, then drop quickly down. This change in your body's chemical balance will adversely affect your mood. Likewise, meals that are hard to digest (like a big steak) use a lot more of the body's energy to break down the food, making you feel more tired and less upbeat.

One of the best ways you can improve your health is by eating foods rich in omega-3 fatty acids. Countless studies have shown that a shortage of omega-3 can increase the likelihood of depression. (In fact, there's a wonderful book full of fascinating research on omega-3 and the mind called *Brain Food: The Natural Cure for Depression*. It's well worth reading.)

I take several capsules of omega-3 daily to maximize my positive moods. You can also get your omega-3 by eating lots of deep-water fish, such as tuna. Growing evidence suggests that taking omega-3 daily can assist your memory and boost your overall brain power, too. It's really quite a magical supplement.

Happiness Booster 5: Control Your Focus

It's not what happens to you in life that makes you happy or sad long term—it's how you react to what happens. By controlling what you think about, you can dramatically alter your mood for the better. With a little daily practice, you can actually train yourself to be more optimistic, hopeful and positive, and when you consistently do this your mood will greatly improve.

Remember: you are always in control of what you allow your mind to focus on. Dwell on the negative aspects of your life (and let's face it—we all have some) and sure enough, you'll feel down. But condition your mind to look for the good in a situation and you'll always feel at least a little bit happier.

One of the most important times to focus on the good is when you think about the future. So many people are apprehensive about the future, expecting the worst. But as we all know from experience, usually the worst doesn't happen. It's far more sensible to train yourself to expect the best—you'll perform better, feel happier, and probably increase the chance of more good things happening in your life. When it comes to enduring happiness, controlling what you focus on is vital.

Happiness Booster 6: Take Action

One of the most depressing situations you can experience is to feel stuck. Whenever you feel like you're not making progress, or you're not in control of your life, you will soon feel unhappy.

The solution is simple: take action. Then take action again, and again, and again—in any area of your life you don't feel good about. Make that call. Visit that place. Create a to-do list, then do something on it. Forgive. Cut off. Object. Get to work. Trust. Move forward in some way.

Taking massive action makes you feel better in two powerful ways. Firstly, the action itself often improves the situation for you—any progress feels good. Secondly, merely taking action makes you feel more in control, and feeling you're in control of your life is usually highly uplifting. Certainly the alternative—helplessness—is almost always depressing. (For more about this, read *Control Theory* by William Glasser.)

If you're feeling stuck right now, make a list of three steps you can take to move forward. Then try to do all three in the next hour.

A MATTER OF BALANCE

Do all six of these happiness boosters and your levels of joy and content-ment will be vastly higher than someone who just looks to money for their happiness.

I think, though, it's safe to say that even knowing all this research, most people will remain somewhat tempted by the lure of cash for the rest of their lives. We're only human, after all. Frankly, there's nothing wrong with pursuing wealth; just don't worship it. Don't let money be your master. Blend your natural ambitions with daily efforts to practice the six Happiness Boosters and you'll be far richer in the long run. After all, surely true wealth is about experiencing genuine and plentiful happiness and companionship; it's not just about a new Mercedes-Benz.

One of life's most remarkable experiences is to travel to a tropical island or a poor African nation and discover that despite owning very little, the inhabitants are usually some of the happiest people you'll see in your entire life. Why? It's simple. They've got a close, caring community, they have great relationships and they're grateful for the things life has given them. If we can learn to think the same as these so-called "primitive natives," then that kind of deep, glowing happiness can also be ours.

not focusing
on strengths

*I believe we have a major learning problem in our society,
worldwide: we focus too much on our weaknesses.*

Western culture applauds people who manage to overcome
their weaknesses and win a victory, however small. We love
hearing stories about the short person who makes the basketball team, the poor math student who graduates with an accounting
degree, or the average writer who still manages to churn out a book. As
a society we greatly admire the unlikely victor, the underdog, the person
who beats the odds.

Now don't get me wrong—I have admiration for any great achievement, I really do. But my point is this: if you're not suited to doing
something, if you are weak at it, why devote hundreds of hours of your
life to doing it? Sure, you might make some progress, even have a win
or two, but is it really the best use of your time? I don't think so, and
growing scientific evidence backs me up.

I really feel we need to change our attitude to weakness—in our schools, in our universities, and even in our families. Instead of focusing on our weaknesses and trying to make them passable, we need to focus on our strengths and make them absolutely superb.

After all, you can spend years working on your weaknesses and at the end of that time the best you'll probably have is some really strong weaknesses! Hardly an exciting result.

But consider a different way to live. Imagine a life spent focusing on all the things you're really talented at, the things you find easier, more interesting, and fun, and then devoting yourself to making those natural talents the very best they can be. Now *that* would be an invigorating life.

It's also likely to be a more successful one. Because you'd be doing something you enjoy, you'd be far more likely to work hard at it, learn as much as you could about it and seek mastery in it. That extra effort and enthusiasm would almost certainly translate into excellent results.

THE SPECIALIST ERA

A strengths-focused life has many benefits. More success. Increased enjoyment. Greater self-confidence and life satisfaction. It really is a better way to live. But you'd be amazed at how few people live this way.

Globally respected strengths expert Marcus Buckingham has found that a paltry 12 percent of people believe their strengths are being used at work most of the time. Many workers use their strengths and real talents for less than an hour a day! No wonder so many people report being bored, frustrated, and generally disenchanted during their work week. If you consider how many hundreds of millions of people are probably not using their strengths at work, you quickly realize what a shocking waste of human capital is occurring. It basically means corporations worldwide are functioning at a fraction of what they could be.

It's easy to see why this way of thinking prevails. For hundreds of years society has admired generalists, people who are quite good at a wide variety of tasks. In medieval times, for instance, someone who could farm the land and make tools was more useful than someone who purely farmed. During the industrial revolution a person who could work a machine as well as do the accounts was valued more than another who was only good with machines. That philosophy remains popular to this day in many companies, but is it really the best way to think?

I suspect not. I believe we have entered the age of the specialist. Life has become so complex that it's impossible to be really, really good at more than one or two aspects of work. Fields of work have become so deep, so varied, so ever-changing that it takes someone's complete focus just to keep up with what's happening in that one area.

In medicine, for example, it is said that the world's medical knowledge is doubling every three years. In business, the Internet has put all our learning curves into overdrive. The globalization of society has meant that we can no longer get by with just knowing what's happening in our own country or industry—we must be aware of what's occurring worldwide.

For all these reasons, being good at many things is becoming a lost art. And it's an unnecessary one. Far more valued nowadays (and certainly more financially rewarding) is the person who is the absolute best in their field in just one important area. It's the specialist lawyer who gets famous. It's the expert in a single area of finance who gets the big bucks. It's the athlete who focuses on one sport, not several, who makes it to the top.

Now here's the problem. I don't believe you can become really excellent, absolutely knock-'em-dead amazing in any field unless you're naturally suited to it—that is, unless it utilizes your strengths. It's just too much hard work to become brilliant at something you dislike or show little talent for. Even if you do manage it, you're almost certain to be surpassed by someone else who worked equally hard but also found the field that suits his or her natural strengths.

We all need to focus on our strengths much more. We then need to build our daily lives around those strengths, so that the majority of our working day is spent doing projects and tasks that we enjoy and that suit our talents. If we do this, both our life satisfaction and our success level will rise tremendously.

THE GALLUP FINDINGS

Much of the pioneering work done on strengths finding was produced inside the Gallup Organization, one of the world's finest research firms. It was led by the "Father of Strengths Psychology," Donald O. Clifton and Tom Rath.

The Gallup team examined more than fifty years of research into human thought and action to work out the top handful of rules that anyone could follow to discover his or her strengths. They discovered some amazing stuff. For example, they found that if you focus on your strengths every day, you are *three times* more likely to report having an excellent quality of life.

They also worked out that if your boss focuses on your weaknesses, your chances of feeling engaged at work are just 1 percent. (Note to bosses: are there people working under you who might feel that you are not focusing on their strengths? Be careful. Those staff may well be looking to work elsewhere, where they feel more appreciated and competent.) Out of the 10 million people they surveyed, a whopping seven million felt they weren't living a strengths-focused life! This is a major issue for the global workplace.

Clifton and Rath calculated that if you are not using your strengths you are *six times* more likely to be disengaged at work. You are subsequently more likely to treat customers poorly, achieve less, have poor interactions with colleagues, and often dread going to work. Yuck.

They also found that it's not just your work life that suffers. Poorer health and lower-quality relationships at home are common among those not in their "strengths zone."

All in all, the evidence is comprehensive and damning. Anyone who doesn't create a life centered around their strengths will experience vastly less success and a demonstrably lower quality of life.

KNOW YOUR STRENGTHS

The crazy thing is, though, that very few of us actually know what our strengths are. Most people have never sat down and done a serious evaluation of what they're good at. Yet to be clear on your talents and to focus on them continually is one of the most effective steps you can take to increase your happiness and success in life.

Do you know what your strengths are? Have you designed your life so that you are focusing on what you are good at and enjoy? Or are you like most people who just go to work every day with almost no attempt to maximize their natural gifts?

Trust me: if you get really clear on your strengths and centre your life around them, you will be living at an exceedingly high level. You'll be more effective, get better results and enjoy your work much more if you know what you're good at and stick to it. Life becomes much smoother and more satisfying when you're doing what you're naturally suited to.

So let's work out what your strengths are right now. In just five minutes from now you will know what you're really good at and how much of your time is spent using your talents. Please grab a pen and answer the following quick quiz.

Strengths Evaluator

1. What three tasks at work do you find easy and interesting?
   1. _____
   2. _____
   3. _____
2. What skills do you need to do those three things well?
   1. _____
   2. _____
   3. _____
3. What were you good at when you were at school?
   1. _____
   2. _____
   3. _____
4. What do your friends think you're good at? (Phone, e-mail, or text them now)

(continued)

Strengths Evaluator (continued)

   1. _____
   2. _____
   3. _____

5. If money weren't an issue, what jobs would you most enjoy doing?
   1. _____
   2. _____
   3. _____

6. What tasks do coworkers think you do better than others?
   1. _____
   2. _____
   3. _____

7. What are your hobbies or nonwork interests?
   1. _____
   2. _____
   3. _____

8. What tasks do you find difficult or stressful?
   1. _____
   2. _____
   3. _____

9. Consider your answers above. Based on that information, what do you believe your top strengths are?
   1. _____
   2. _____
   3. _____

10. Based on all your answers, what do you believe your weaknesses are?
   1. _____
   2. _____
   3. _____

11. Finally, how much time do you estimate you spend on your strengths most work days?
   1. _____
   2. _____
   3. _____

I think you'll agree it's a fascinating questionnaire. Most people find that once they ask themselves these questions, they actually find it quite easy to work out what their strengths are. It's just that in many cases they've never actually spent the time asking such questions. Remember: the first key to greatness is self-knowledge.

The question that usually yields the most surprising answer is the last one. Lots of folks are amazed to discover just how little time each day is spent doing projects that they are good at or enjoy. Many of us have convinced ourselves that that's just how life is, that work is supposed to be boring most of the time. But it doesn't have to be this way. You can make small changes in your present job that will dramatically increase your enjoyment, progress, and prosperity.

FURTHER KNOWLEDGE

If you found doing my quick Strengths Evaluator useful, the Gallup Organization has an hour-long test that more deeply investigates what your personal strengths are. This is named the Clifton Strengths Finder in honor of the late Donald Clifton. Over two million people all over the world have completed this comprehensive strengths quiz. It's available in 24 languages and can be modified for people with disabilities.

The test has been very useful for companies. Research indicates that when employees do the Clifton Strengths Finder and get the feedback from it, they feel more engaged at work and productivity rises 12.5 percent on average. In addition, retail stores whose managers got this feedback on their strengths increased their profits by an average of 8.9 percent! That's how important knowledge of our strengths can be.

Another excellent test to help you define your strengths is the Kolbe Index. It's a simple online questionnaire that takes less than half an hour to complete, yet is highly revealing. Within a minute of completing it the website presents you with a series of charts that analyze what you're good at and what you should avoid doing as much as possible.

I did the Kolbe Index several years ago and regularly pop onto the site to review my results to ensure I'm doing the things I have most aptitude for. I highly recommend it. (Note that there is a charge for taking the test.)

ENVISION A NEW FUTURE

Take a moment to imagine a different life. Think about a scenario where you spend maybe five or six hours every day doing stuff you get a kick out of. If you could design such a life, don't you think you'd enjoy work a whole lot more? I don't think there's any doubt about it.

It's not an impossible dream, either. With a little creative thinking up front (and perhaps some time spent winning a few people over to your way of thinking), I believe you can create that lifestyle within a few weeks.

The first step is to be fully aware of what your strengths are and the amount of time you currently spend engaging those strengths. The next step is to get together with your boss, coworkers, lover, or family and negotiate a way of working and living that not only fulfils your needs, but also handles their needs as well. The two should go together. After all, if you're happier and more productive, that will usually be a good result for them, too.

Once you've reached agreement on how you can spend your day centered around strengths-based activities, it's vital that you design a weekly program to make sure you live this way consistently. Remember: what you systematize tends to happen, and what you leave up in the air tends to be pushed out of your life by more urgent, easier, or more expedient activities.

FOUR HOURS IS ENOUGH

At the beginning of each week write into your diary at least four hours a day of activities that use your strengths. That still leaves most of the day free for other things. By putting in your strengths-based tasks early in the week, you will increase the chances that you'll get them done.

In fact, I bet that after just two weeks of following such a program your life will be revolutionized. You'll be doing two, three, even five times more strengths-based activities once you write them in your diary each week in advance. Then, as you start achieving more of the things that matter and doing more of what you're good at, you'll feel a surge of happiness and satisfaction rise within you. We just plain feel better when our days are focused around our strengths.

If you really, truly don't think you can design four hours a day working with your strengths, then set yourself the target of doing at least three major strengths-based activities each week. It doesn't seem like much, but just watch how your life improves when you do this. You'll feel empowered, uplifted, and vastly more self-confident. Every Monday morning, take five minutes to set aside some blocks of time in your diary to do your three strengths-based activities. On the following Monday, before you write down your next three, take a moment to review how well you did the previous week. Be tough on yourself—this weekly strengths-based stuff is important.

This new way of working will soon become a self-reinforcing loop. As you do better work, you'll feel better about yourself and your life. As you feel better about yourself, your self-esteem will rise. As your self-esteem goes up, so will your performance. And so it goes around. Centering your work around your strengths is one of the greatest secrets to a high-quality life. Yet very few people focus daily on making sure they're doing what they really get a kick out of and show aptitude for.

BE FLEXIBLE BUT FIRM

The stark reality is that there will still be times when an unexpected meeting or task is forced on you and your strengths-based blocks of time get pushed aside for the day. That's OK. Just make sure the next morning you're back to implementing your program, and the week will still be profitable and enjoyable. The trick is to get back on track as soon as possible.

Expect a bit of friction when you first begin to implement your weekly program, too. Some people around you won't like the fact that you're getting serious about maximizing your time. Those of your friends and associates who are used to interrupting you whenever they feel like it or who prefer to live their lives in a more unstructured, free-wheeling way may object at first to your new system. Be a bit flexible to accommodate their needs, but balance that with a decent dose of firmness. It's your life, and you have the right to design it in a way that maximizes both your achievement and your pleasure.

It's been my experience, though, that after a few weeks of standing firm on your commitment, most people in your life get the message and adapt to your schedule.

Once you've got your strengths-based weekly plan up and running smoothly, consider helping two or three other people in your company or personal life to create their own program. It's not just a nice thing to do—having the people around you functioning at such a high level will help lift your life as well. When they're more productive and happier, you will be too.

Imagine a world where everyone in your close community is living a strengths-based life. If you could get 10 people around you operating at this level it would really be something special. Just think of the collective life-satisfaction levels of the group. It's possible to make it happen. It just takes the initial education, mixed with a little patience and time.

Like many of the techniques I recommend in this book, this one relies on you remembering to focus on it. So once again I advocate leaving a simple reminder note on your kitchen bench or computer keyboard, or perhaps a permanent message on your computer's screensaver.

Another useful technique is to write down your three best strengths and three worst weaknesses and make sure they're somewhere where you view them often. Marcus Buckingham suggests reading them at least once a day to keep them right at the front of your mind.

GREAT FOR KIDS

Working out key strengths is a wonderful exercise to do with your kids as well. As long as they've reached, say, 15 or 16 years old, they (and you) will probably have a pretty good idea of what they are good at and enjoy. Rather than let them become depressed about school subjects they take no pleasure in, introduce them to the strengths concept and assure them that even if they're having terrible trouble with particular subjects, they are still high-grade people—they just have strengths and weaknesses like everybody else.

Moving a kid to a strengths-based life is one of the greatest gifts you can possibly give them. It usually immediately makes them feel better about themselves and gets them excited about living a life of excellence, doing activities they love and are good at. Their self-esteem rises quickly. Of course, while they're at school they'll still have to do subjects they don't like. But knowing they have strengths they will always be able to rely on in life will help them do the tough classes while remaining confident about their abilities and self-worth.

NOT JUST FOR YOU

By the way, if you are a company owner or team leader, it would be wise to make sure all your staff have done a strengths test. It will make a massive difference to both the productivity and the morale of your group. Once you know the natural strengths of each member of your team, you can place them in jobs they are really suited to and will enjoy much more. This will raise their self-esteem and inevitably make them feel more engaged at work.

As a leader, what you should be aiming for is a company or group where everyone involved is doing what they're really good at. It's not easy, and let's face it: there will always be times when we have to do tasks we don't like. But it is highly possible to design a workplace where people are largely involved in activities that use their strengths. I'm sure you'll agree.

GENUINE LIFE IMPROVEMENT

I find it very exciting that we can all have access to tests and tools that comprehensively reveal our strengths and then provide powerful steps we can take to use these strengths more in our daily life. The research suggests that both our happiness and our success will lift up to new levels when we know and apply our strengths. It's such a simple thing to do, yet it can dramatically improve the quality of millions of people's lives.

To live a life centered around your strengths is central to avoiding failure in life. Yet so very few people have a really tight handle on what their innate strengths actually are. As a result, they often end up utilizing those strengths for just a handful of hours each week when they could be breezing through work and life if they concentrated on what they excel at and enjoy.

Please don't make this mistake. Review my Strengths Evaluator questionnaire a few pages back, or take the time to do the complete Clifton Strengths Finder test. Then sit down and work out a straightforward weekly program that enables you to spend most of your days focused around your strengths.

If you do, the quality of your life will improve within days.

conclusion

Wow, what a journey! Throughout the book we've seen that failure doesn't just happen—it almost always has reasons behind it. Looking back on any failure, you can almost always work out different things you could have done to avoid it or at least to reduce the severity of its impact.

We've also discovered that there are simple but powerful steps you can take to virtually eliminate long-term failure in your life. You can design your life so that the inevitable low moments are kept to a minimum and the high ones are maximized.

Let's briefly review the 16 reasons people fail and what you can do to eliminate them.

1. UNCLEAR PURPOSE

Focus is crucial. If you are unclear about the purpose of your life, then your day-to-day actions will often be wishy-washy and weak. Without an overall life purpose to guide you like a golden compass, you will get caught up worrying about the trivial and the urgent, not the important. The ridiculously busy world we live in will ensure that you fill your days handling the requests and dreams of other people, rather than creating your own.

But if you choose a major and definite life purpose and build your life around it, working each day to bring your vision closer and closer to reality, then the quality of life you experience escalates significantly. Choices become clearer, problems resolve themselves, answers become quickly apparent. When you have a clear and inspiring life purpose, every department of life becomes easier.

If you're having trouble selecting your life purpose, my advice is to just choose one from the shortlist that you completed earlier and try it on for six months. The truth is that if you are having trouble choosing between two life directions it usually means both purposes are good. Just choose one. Simply having a life purpose will so quickly improve your life it would be a crime against yourself to let it remain undecided for even one more day. Choose one and move forward!

2. DESTRUCTIVE THINKING

What you think about each day has a huge impact on how well you perform and how happy you are. But many of us have never considered that we can be the masters of our thoughts—we can control them and direct them in ways that support and uplift us, rather than drop an anchor on our life.

I absolutely believe that one of the greatest moments of a person's life is the moment they decide to no longer be a victim of their destructive thinking and commit to taking charge of their thoughts. From that moment on, that person's quality of life improves dramatically.

It's anything but easy. I've been working on my thinking for decades and like anyone else I still have times when I'm down and negative. But I honestly believe the thinking and focusing techniques I've discussed in this book can improve how positively you think. I use them all the time and anyone who knows me will tell you that I am almost always positive, uplifted, and enjoying life. That doesn't just happen. It's largely a result of daily mind training.

3. LOW PRODUCTIVITY

In the end, success or failure all comes down to your actions. You can have the best life vision in the world and mountains of brilliant ideas, but if you don't act on them you may as well have never even thought of them.

People who fail usually don't take enough action. They think too much and do too little. Even when they do act consistently, they often don't act intelligently. The heart of intelligent action is to try something, evaluate how it went, adjust your strategy, then try again. Doing the same thing over and over when it's clearly not working will just depress and deplete you.

Productivity is simple:

1. Get clear about what you want.
2. Take action.
3. Change your approach if it isn't working, and stick with it if it is.

Add the techniques of doing the most important action first and working in uninterrupted blocks of time and you'll be more productive than 99 percent of the people on the planet. Really.

High productivity—how some people can do a week's work in a day and still leave the office early—is an exciting field that I find fascinating. I'm determined to learn and master the art of productivity at the very highest level and I urge you to do the same.

4. FIXED MINDSET

There are two mindsets you can have: fixed mindset and growth mindset. When you have a fixed mindset you are fearful of venturing into new areas and greatly concerned about what other people think of you. This attitude tends to inhibit your activities, making you play safe and not stretch your boundaries. Because we live in an ever-progressing world, that mindset slowly causes you to be left behind in both your career and your personal evolution.

But all is not lost. You can change. You can consciously develop a growth mindset and almost immediately improve your results and effectiveness. Those with a growth mindset value learning and progress over just about anything else. As a result of continued growth in every field of life that they value, people with a growth mindset are always getting better and more adept at the things they work on. Progress and growth feel good, thus their mood is usually better and their self-esteem is higher. It's not just a more efficacious way to live—it's a hell of a lot more fun, too.

5. WEAK ENERGY

We often forget that the human body is a machine. Like any machine it needs to be maintained well and powered by a quality energy source. If you're neglecting your energy levels, then eventually you will fail, or at the very least perform at a mediocre level.

I see many corporate executives who think they don't have time to eat well, sleep well, or generally look after themselves. They're too busy "getting things done." The absurd reality is that there's loads of research that shows they'd get a whole lot more done if they actually took time off and made the effort to make sure their energy levels remained high and strong, rather than just working night and day.

Energy matters. It's crucial to long-term success. It's also a vital component of happiness—when you have loads of physical energy you usually feel strong mentally, too. What are you doing today to increase your energy levels? Together, natural foods, vigorous exercise, regulated sleep, and daily meditation to relieve stress will work wonders.

6. NOT ASKING THE RIGHT QUESTIONS

It's so easy to drift through life, reacting to what happens to you rather than pausing to ask the questions that matter. The fact is, the quality of your life depends on the quality of questions you regularly ask yourself.

In Chapter Six I listed some of the key questions I ask myself often—when I'm stuck, stressed, looking for opportunities, or trying to break out of traditional thinking. I've found them tremendously helpful when I've been feeling a little down, too. They get me thinking forward instead of staying stuck in the mental quicksand of my present-day situation.

Give them a try. Keep the list on a piece of paper in a nearby drawer, ready to be taken out and read whenever you need some help with your future direction. And of course, feel free to add to my list with powerful questions of your own. When it comes to constructive, effective thinking, questions are the answer.

7. POOR PRESENTATION SKILLS

Like it or not, we live in a shallow world. People are often judged by their appearance. If you can't present well, then you will fail in your endeavors regularly. Remember: nothing big happens until someone sells someone else on something, whether it's an idea, a product, a service, or a person.

There's no use decrying this attitude—it's just how life is. The only solution is to get good at presenting as fast as you can.

I've shown you some highly effective techniques to quickly improve your presentation ability. But if you only read them, they'll be of little help to you. You have to set a time every week for a month when you spend time practicing your presenting. Get friends to judge your performance. Videotape it yourself and watch it over and over again, the way all top sports stars review their games.

Great presenters are usually made, not born. Become excellent at this one skill and the quality of your life will rise dramatically. Guaranteed. You will scarcely find a single successful person in business who isn't at least OK as a presenter. And in social situations, the person who presents well has a clear advantage over others.

8. MISTAKING IQ FOR EQ

The identification of Emotional Intelligence, or EQ for short, is one of the most important breakthroughs in modern mind science. Even though a person's IQ test score has for decades been considered the most accurate indicator of their mental power, the new EQ research shows a totally different story. Our emotional wisdom—our empathy for others, our self-discipline, our optimism, and our ability to get along with those around us—has a far higher impact on our success or failure in life.

Truth be told, the importance of IQ is greatly overrated. That's very fortunate for most of us, because it's hard to improve an IQ score. But EQ can be improved within weeks, if you do two things.

First, get clear on where you score well on EQ and which EQ areas you can improve on. And second, make a few small efforts every week to get better in your problem areas. The rewards are substantial: better relationships, a quicker rise up the career ladder— even your health is likely to improve when you develop a strong EQ level.

9. POOR SELF-IMAGE

You don't meet many failures who see themselves as successful. Our self-image and our performance are strongly aligned. The great news, though, is that there are several potent ways to improve your self-image, and thus your performance. Visualize that you're successful for at least a few minutes every day. Remind yourself of your successes each evening before you sleep. Speak to yourself positively and be your own mind coach (I give myself a pep talk as I'm driving to the gym in the morning—I look crazy, but it works). Replace negative ways with positive ones. It's easier than you think.

A bad self-image doesn't just grow inside your brain by accident. It's a result of what you consistently and habitually think. You can change that—you really can. But you must discipline yourself to dedicate at least a few minutes every day to making the change occur. Have you written a time in your diary each day to cultivate a strong self-image? Believe me: your life will change when you do.

10. NOT ENOUGH THINKING

It's the disease of modern society—the never-ending race to constantly do stuff, rather than think deeply and then do. And it's only getting worse. Failures are just as busy as successes, but they are taking actions that are often a waste of time. Successful people resist the urge to leap into action without forethought; instead, they carefully plan their line of attack.

I remember talking to my wife, Kathryn Eisman, about how she managed to score at the top of her class in her final school exams. Kathryn said her secret was simple: while everyone else in the exam room rushed to start their essays as soon as the exam began, she spent the first five minutes planning what she would write, thinking of ideas and arguments that would form the heart of her essay. Up-front thinking and planning made a tremendous difference to the quality of her results, and will do the same for you.

Taking the time to really think things through is a common trait in winners and usually missing in losers. Dedicating hours, days or even weeks to conceiving breakthrough ideas is a vital part of achieving uncommon success.

We must all fight the feeling that we are only being useful when we're doing stuff. Often it's quality thinking that is the difference that makes the difference.

11. NO DAILY RITUALS

This is one of the top reasons people fail. It's also hardly ever mentioned in self-development or high-performance books. You can have the best intentions in the world—you can even start off powering towards your goals—but if you don't establish daily action rituals, it's highly likely you'll run out of steam before you achieve what you're aiming for.

Rituals are at the heart of any effective success system. By developing a series of activities that become habit and therefore don't require huge effort to do, you make progress toward your goals every week. If, however, your actions are random and you leave your dreams to a time when you're free, or in between other tasks, your progress will be slow and your motivation will weaken.

12. STRESS

Stress is far more dangerous than most of us realize. It's the common factor behind numerous diseases, broken relationships, and bouts of depression. It's also a major cause of failure.

Never forget, though: it's not what happens to you that makes you stressed, it's how you react to what happens. It may not feel like it sometimes, but you are always in control of your stress levels, because you are ultimately in control of your thoughts. Discipline yourself to see the upside in every situation (no matter how terrible it may seem). Discipline yourself to mentally release your tension at the end of each and every day (if you don't, your stress levels will inevitably build over time). Discipline yourself to create breaks throughout the day and relaxing activities at night and on weekends. It can be done. It must be done. Stress is just too dangerous for you to allow it into your life unchallenged.

Follow the strategies for stress reduction I've outlined in this book and you will see a phenomenal lowering of your stress levels. I regularly use these techniques and can absolutely vouch for their effectiveness. They work wonders. And with society not slowing down anytime soon, you owe it to yourself to make them a part of your life and reap the benefits.

13. FEW RELATIONSHIPS

We can't achieve success at any significant level without the assistance of others. Highly successful people always develop a crack team of advisers to help them reach their goals. The fact is, you are only as good as the team around you.

But relationships aren't just important for your professional success—they're even more vital for your personal success. Life can be grueling at times, and when the road gets a little rocky it's imperative you have a support system of people who care about you, to help you navigate through those rough patches. Here's the key: you have to develop these relationships *before* you need them. You need to have put enough deposits in their emotional bank account so that when you one day call upon them in your hour of need, they are more than willing to help you. By creating deep relationships, you will soon build up a mighty fortress of work and life friends who can come to your aid and help you reach your dreams.

14. LACK OF PERSISTENCE

The great myth about successful people is that they are just more talented. But this simply isn't true in most cases. It may not be glamorous, but the fact is that most people get ahead of the pack by simply trying harder, working longer, doing more, and basically just persisting longer than the average failure. Often the only thing that sets the super-successes apart from the also-rans in life is their sheer dogged determination to keep on going until they make it.

Our society and schooling system need to emphasize the power of persistence over talent far more than they currently do. We need to put persistence right at the top of the list of character traits to develop, because at the end of the day, behind all those exciting stories of the mega-successful, you'll usually find that good old, down-and-dirty persistence was the real secret to their stardom.

So push yourself. Go the extra mile. Make persistence part of your self-image. Then watch how good your luck becomes.

15. MONEY OBSESSION

Materialism is at epidemic levels and still rising fast in many countries. So many of us are obsessed with getting more, more, more, rather than enjoying what we've already got. And what we've got is plenty—research shows that, in the developed world, the average person's real wealth has increased dramatically since the 1950s. As a society we are the richest we've been in history. The trouble is our expectations have risen too, so we are also demanding to get more than ever. That endless grasping for more virtually ensures a feeling of failure.

Now don't get me wrong—I'm all for wealth. After all, money is really only a payment for service that you've rendered to other people. But building your entire life around the accumulation of money is a sure road to misery. The latest happiness research conclusively confirms it: putting money or fame first in your life leads to less happiness, poorer health, less community involvement, and lower self-esteem. If that's not a failed life I don't know what is.

So don't fall for materialistic temptations. Build your life around relationships, community, serving others, and appreciation, and all the research says you will have a far more enjoyable time than the money worshippers.

16. NOT FOCUSING ON STRENGTHS

You are special. Really special. You have a unique combination of abilities unmatched by anyone else on the planet. You are also pretty terrible at some things. Hey, no one's perfect. Rather than try to make your weaknesses into strengths, it's far smarter to design your life (as much as you can) around your strengths.

But this is not what most people do. The majority spend only a handful of hours each day doing things that use their strengths. Most of the day is spent engaging in activities that they're average at, or downright terrible at doing.

Now obviously you may not be able to spend your entire day doing work centered around your natural strengths. But the more you do, the more successful (and joyful) your life will be.

You know life is short. Don't spend it doing things that you are neither good at nor particularly enjoy. Anyone can re-create their life so that they are doing more things that enrich and nurture them, and that they have a talent for. All that's needed is the will to make it happen.

A FORMULA FOR CHANGE

Those are the main 16 reasons that people fail. Look at anyone you know who is not succeeding, and you will find not just one but several of these failure signs occurring in their life.

But hey, don't be too hard on yourself if you have a few of them—we all do at various times of our life. It's really normal and totally OK. What isn't OK, though, is to not try to rid your life of these failure mechanisms once you've identified them. (To watch a video of me being interviewed about the 16 obstacles to success, visit www.whypeoplefail.org.)

Not one of the 16 causes of failure needs to be permanent—they are all fixable. You don't have to have them in your life.

The formula for getting rid of them is simple, too:

1. Identify which of the failure causes you have.
2. Design a ritual to overcome them.
3. Do something every day, no matter how small, that gets you closer to victory.

Long term, you simply cannot fail at life if you follow this formula. I really don't think that God set up life for us to lose. Mother Nature and the higher powers want us to win and be happy—I genuinely believe that. But life didn't come with an instruction book. We have to learn how to be victorious by ourselves. That's the exciting (and sometimes exasperating!) challenge we all must face.

Learning these lessons can be very tough sometimes, but the laws themselves aren't complex. Believe in yourself. Serve people every day. Tell the truth. Be caring. Work hard. Stay healthy. Be grateful. Strive for excellence. Connect to a higher power. Keep learning. Have fun. Is there much more to a successful life than that? Well, to me, that's about all there is to it.

The challenge comes, of course, when you forget the rules. And it's so easy to do. That's why you have to do everything you can to keep those laws at the top of your mind. When you read them every day, ponder them, make them a part of your daily life, then you usually make them happen—and life starts to favor you.

This is your mission, and mine. To live life with clarity. To focus on what counts. To take time to reflect on how you're travelling and quietly adjust and improve your approach. It's as much about mental work (and often spiritual work) as it is about physical tasks. The simple truth is that if you don't spend time tending the garden of your mind, then weeds will surely grow there. It doesn't take a huge amount of effort to keep your mind clean, healthy, and positive, but it must be done daily. You must have a ritual.

COMMIT TO YOUR EVOLUTION

In the material world life is developing at an astonishingly quick pace. Society is evolving faster than ever before. Just make sure your inner world is evolving too, or all of those material-world battles will leave you feeling left behind and out of control.

This is a wonderful time in history to be alive. Absolute poverty is declining (that's a statistically proven fact), the world is largely at peace, huge parts of the globe are moving from the third world to the developed world (India and China, to name but two). All in all, things are looking pretty good.

Even more important, our knowledge of the power that dwells inside each and every one of us is growing at a rapid pace, too. I feel a real sense that we have reached a tipping point in human consciousness. We are collectively beginning to understand the massive potential we each have as human beings. The potential to become better, wiser, stronger, healthier, and happier is being revealed daily by scientists, spiritual masters, mind researchers, and our own experiences. We are realizing that each of us is someone really, really special.

So as our time together comes to an end, I leave you with the following thought.

Even a thousand years from now, humankind will not have fully uncovered the tremendous powers that lie inside each individual. We are not only more than we think we are, we are far greater than many of us can even imagine in our wildest dreams. I believe that at the core of our being, we are all supermen and superwomen. The greatest challenge of life is not just to make money, have fun, and then die; it is to look within and unlock these mighty powers.

One of the most life-changing things you can ever do is to switch your aim in life from acquiring and enjoying to opening up your higher human powers. This, I believe, is the grandest adventure of them all, and will provide greater riches than you can imagine.

In my own very small way, I am committed to travelling this golden road.

Will you join me?

recommended reading

The Power of Full Engagement by Jim Loehr and Tony Schwartz

A masterly treatise on the science of lasting achievement, centered on the premise that energy, not time, is the main determinant of high performance. Unless your spiritual, physical, mental, and emotional energies are strongly aligned, you are not performing at your optimum.

Flow: The Psychology of Optimal Experience by Mihaly Csikszentmihalyi

A book that has made many readers review their concept of enjoyment. Are you most happy doing little, just relaxing? Professor Csikszentmihalyi argues persuasively against that theory. True enjoyment arises when you are fully engaged in an activity, your capacities stretched, losing track of time.

Think Like a Winner by Yehuda Shinar

A smart analysis of peak performance from one of Israel's most renowned winning coaches. Shinar has worked with everyone from air force pilots to pro football teams, and his experience shows. His thinking models are simple and useful.

How the Best Get Better by Dan Sullivan
> A short, sharp instruction manual from an excellent entrepreneurial coach. There are more valuable strategies in this slim book than in most other books 10 times the size.

Tao Te Ching by Lao Tzu
> An ancient text that has reportedly been translated more times than any other book except the Bible. In it, the ex-librarian turned philosopher Lao Tzu explains how you can achieve lasting success by emulating the way nature behaves. A timeless masterpiece.

Talent Is Never Enough by John C. Maxwell
> Maxwell is one of the world's most prolific leadership writers, and certainly one of the best. Here he explains that talent is just the start of success. Equally (if not more) important are character traits like initiative, passion, focus, teachability, and perseverance.

The 8th Habit by Stephen R. Covey
> Many have read Dr Covey's brilliant book *The 7 Habits of Highly Effective People*. Fifteen years later, he followed it with another masterwork. It's all about the importance of discovering your voice and then making vision, discipline, passion, and conscience central aspects of your life.

The Element: How Finding Your Passion Changes Everything by Ken Robinson
> One of the most popular speakers at the famous TED Conference in Monterey in the United States, Sir Ken Robinson is delightfully inspiring in this work. He implores us to blend our talents with our passion, no matter what those around us say or think about it.

Get the Life You Want by Richard Bandler
> Heard of neurolinguistic programming, or NLP? Bandler is the cocreator of that highly regarded science of change. Though his

earlier books may have been a bit esoteric for some, this one is really easy to understand and contains some fantastic techniques to help you quickly dump self-defeating habits and ways of thinking.

Feeling Good by David D. Burns

In a national survey, *Feeling Good* was voted the most helpful book on depression out of 1,000 books on the subject. It's easy to see why. It's clear, authoritative, and full of simple cognitive techniques to improve your mood fast. Incredibly, studies have shown that 70 percent of depressed people who read this book improved within four weeks, with no other treatment.

Halftime by Bob Buford

A successful entrepreneur, Buford was forced to reevaluate his life values when his son drowned in a raging river. One result was this magnificent book. Its credo is that your midlife should be a time to reexamine what you really want your life to stand for. Buford urges us to switch our primary life aim from success to significance.

The High Price of Materialism by Tim Kasser

A short book with a big impact. Kasser eruditely shows how our materialistic culture is quietly hurting our chances of happiness and well-being. Deeply researched, it's a wake-up call for the money obsessed.

How Full Is Your Bucket? by Tom Rath and Donald O. Clifton

This book has changed a lot of lives. It proves beyond a doubt that the key to a happy life, good career, and strong relationships is to uplift others rather than focus on their negatives.

Maximum Achievement by Brian Tracy

Tracy has written over forty books on achievement, but this was his first. It's a comprehensive examination of the mental aspects of success. There are excellent chapters on the laws of mental mastery and the power of goal setting.

Unlimited Power by Anthony Robbins
A breakthrough in the self-improvement field when first published, Robbins' first book is still one of the most comprehensive sources of quality personal development techniques around. It is rich in science and saturated with the author's most marked character trait: passion.

The Seven Spiritual Laws of Success by Deepak Chopra
A slender volume that has transformed many people's understanding of wealth accumulation. Despite its brevity, it remains one of the most profound books ever written on success manifestation and is the perfect success book for those with an interest in the spiritual realms.

The Leadership Challenge by Jim Kouzes and Barry Posner
A definitive classic with over one and a half million copies in print. Kouzes & Posner have dedicated 30 years of research to defining effective leadership, and the accessible principles in this book are still the best roadmap for leading well. Highly recommended.

acknowledgments

Many people have helped me complete this book, either through their direct professional assistance or indirect personal support.

Thanks to Brian Sher, for his wise advice and big thinking. To Bradley Greive for his inspiring attitude of going for it on a worldwide scale. To my personal assistant, Tania, for her years of loyalty and excellence. To the boys—Johnny, Mike, Elvis, Chris, the EO boys, Phil, and Ghassy—I treasure our friendship. To Marrianne, Cicada, Ari and Ben, Tang, Basquali, the wonderfully welcoming Eisman clan, and the Packhams—you all have made my life so much richer.

Muchas gracias to the team at Jossey Bass—my wonderful editor Genoveva Llosa, my patient production editor Michael Kay, John Maas, Adrian Morgan, Meredith Stanton, and Erin Moy. Your tireless efforts behind the scenes are deeply appreciated.

Of course, this book would never have happened without the tireless work of my superb literary agent, Al Zukerman. Thanks again Al.

And finally, thanks to my darling Kath. Your pure love, wise counsel, and joyful spirit have taught me so much about what being a true success is all about.

the author

S iimon Reynolds is a mentor to business leaders, worldwide. He has won numerous awards for business and career success. Siimon is the cofounder of Photon Group, which in eight years grew from two people to over 6,000, becoming the fifteenth largest marketing services group in the world, with operations in fourteen countries. Today Siimon travels the world speaking on personal and business achievement, as well as personally coaching a select group of executives and entrepreneurs. A best-selling author, Siimon's books have been published in ten countries. He resides in Los Angeles, California.

If you would like to receive Siimon's acclaimed e-newsletter on high achievement, visit www.whypeoplefail.org and www.siimonreynolds .com, where you'll also find comprehensive information on Siimon's inspiring books, keynote speeches, personal coaching, and seminars.

Siimon offers a range of services for people and corporations looking to maximize their performance:

- Keynote Speeches and Workshops
  Siimon is a highly regarded keynote speaker and seminar leader who delivers inspiring and practical content on:

- High achievement in turbulent times
- Extraordinary productivity and efficiency
- The mindset of the ultra-successful
- Systems for personal excellence

    His audiences leave uplifted and highly motivated to take their corporate and personal performance to an ever higher level.

- Executive Coaching

    Siimon personally coaches a small number of company founders and CEOs on how to finesse their performance, increase profits, achieve more in less time, lead with maximum effectiveness, and balance their work and personal lives. Coaching occurs in person, by phone, and by e-mail.

- Website and Blog

    Stay in touch with Siimon's latest thoughts by subscribing to his blog and e-newsletter. You can join by visiting www.whypeoplefail.org and www.siimonreynolds.com, where you'll find a dynamic collection of leadership and high-performance products and resources.